ABOUT THE AUTHOR

Lyn Klug combines career, marriage, and parenthood. A graduate of St. Olaf College in Northfield, Minnesota, she is a piano teacher and writer, is active in community theatre and area choral groups, and directs the junior choir at her church.

She is the author of *I Know I Can Trust You, Lord*, a prayer book for girls, and together with her husband Ron, is coauthor of *Bible Readings for Parents* and several children's books—*Jesus Comes; Jesus Loves; Jesus Lives!; Please, God;* and *Thank You, God.* In addition, Ron and Lyn Klug are coeditors of *The Christian Family Bedtime Reading Book* and *The Christian Family Christmas Book.*

Lyn and Ron served for four years as educators at a school for missionary children in Madagascar. They now live in Northfield, Minnesota, with their three children, Rebecca, Paul, and Hans.

BIBLE READINGS SERIES

Bible Readings for Women
Lyn Klug
Bible Readings for Men
Steve Swanson
Bible Readings for Parents
Ron and Lyn Klug
Bible Readings for Couples
Margaret and Erling Wold
Bible Readings for Singles
Ruth Stenerson
Bible Readings for Families
Mildred and Luverne Tengbom
Bible Readings for Teenagers
Charles S. Mueller
Bible Readings for Mothers
Mildred Tengbom
Bible Readings for Teachers
Ruth Stenerson
Bible Readings for Students
Ruth Stenerson
Bible Readings for the Retired
Leslie F. Brandt
Bible Readings for Church Workers
Harry N. Huxhold
Bible Readings for Office Workers
Lou Ann Good
Bible Readings for Growing Christians
Kevin E. Ruffcorn
Bible Readings for Caregivers
Betty Groth Syverson
Bible Readings for Troubled Times
Leslie F. Brandt
Bible Readings for Farm Living
Frederick Baltz
Bible Readings on Prayer
Ron Klug
Bible Readings on Hope
Roger C. Palms
Bible Readings on God's Creation
Denise J. Williamson

Bible
Readings
FOR
WOMEN

Bible Readings

FOR
WOMEN

•

Lyn Klug

AUGSBURG Publishing House • Minneapolis

BIBLE READINGS FOR WOMEN

Scripture quotations unless otherwise noted are from the Holy Bible: New International Version. Copyright 1978 by the New York International Bible Society. Used by permission of Zondervan Bible Publishers.

Scripture quotations marked TEV are from the Good News Bible, Today's English Version, copyright 1966, 1971, 1976 by American Bible Society. Used by permission.

Library of Congress Cataloging in Publication Data

Klug, Lyn.
  BIBLE READINGS FOR WOMEN.

  1. Women—Prayer-books and devotions—English.
I. Title.
BV4844.K58   1985   242'.643   85-7508
ISBN 0-8066-2163-X

Manufactured in the U.S.A.   APH 10-0687

9   0   1   2   3   4   5   6   7   8   9

*To the friends who have
shared their lives with me*

PREFACE

Women today face an unprecedented range of opportunities and choices—in careers, family life, finances, politics, relationships, social responsibility, and spirituality. These choices are both exhilarating and confusing.

In our quest, as Christian women we turn again to the Bible and find new light coming from these ancient words. As Jesus promised, the Holy Spirit leads us into truth.

In this book, I have tried to share some of the light I have discovered as I have searched the Bible and other books, old and new, and as I have reflected on my own life as a wife, mother, teacher, friend, and community member. Many of the ideas come from conversations with friends—married, single, and divorced—in which we've struggled with the challenges and shared the joys of our lives. I want to thank them all for their help—both with this book and with my life.

Many women today are sensitive to the masculine bias in much of our language—including our religious vocabulary. I have tried to write in a language all women will be comfortable with. I have chosen, however, to let quotations from the Bible and other books stand as they were written.

My prayer for you is that in these daily readings you will find insight, comfort, and strength as you live as God's woman in God's world for God's purposes.

■ THE THREE JOURNEYS

Heb. 10:23-25: "Let us not give up meeting together, as some are in the habit of doing, but let us encourage one another" (v. 25).

Life can be thought of as a threefold journey. First, there is the journey *inward*. The inward journey is my attempt to find my deepest, truest self—and to offer that self to God and to his purposes. This journey may include prayer, Bible study, meditation, reading, reflecting, journal keeping, solitude, and retreats. From a deep and rich inner life, I gain strength and direction for the journey *outward*.

The journey outward involves all the ways I bring God's love to others in the world. It begins close to home with my own family, church, and community. It may also include whatever I do to work for world peace, or to bring food and medical care to the needy, or to help those who suffer from injustice and tyranny around the globe.

To find a balance between the two journeys, I need a third—the *shared* journey. I need a small group of fellow seekers with whom I can share my struggles and my successes. It's impossible to be a Christian alone. With these few friends, I study, reflect, and pray, as we try to live out our faith in our daily lives.

Together these three journeys are my way of loving God, other people, and myself.

 Thank you, God, for the people you have given me for the shared journey. Help me to encourage them, as they do me.

Is there someone who needs you to share her journey?

■ BUSY WOMEN

Luke 10:38-42: "Only one thing is needed. Mary has chosen what is better, and it will not be taken away from her" (v. 42).

Because Martha is really concerned about social issues, her life is full of church meetings and activities. It seems like she is always in motion.

Mary likes to read, and she enjoys putting on a tape and lying quietly to listen. She goes to a Bible class and belongs to a prayer group.

Our world is full of Marys and Marthas. Sometimes they have a hard time understanding one another. Most of us are probably part Mary and part Martha.

Jesus did not rebuke Martha because she was working, but because she was worried and anxious. That can easily happen when we become so busy, even with worthwhile things, that we fail to take time to renew our contact with God. Listening to the teaching of Jesus is not an escape from the world and its problems; it's a way to grow in compassion, a way to find the strength and guidance we need to make our faith active. That's why Jesus said it is the one thing needed.

 Lord, help me to take time from my busyness to renew my relationship with you. Let me come from this time refreshed and strengthened for service to others.

Are you more of a Mary or a Martha? What do you need to do to have a better balance between the Mary and Martha parts of you?

■ IS SELF-ESTEEM ENOUGH?

1 John 3:1-10: "How great is the love the Father has lavished on us, that we should be called children of God" (v. 1).

The paperback racks are full of books that tell you how to love yourself, how to take care of Number One, how to feel good about yourself.

Feeling glad to be alive, wishing our own happiness, and feeling good because we have been useful are healthy forms of self-esteem. But as William Kirk Kilpatrick writes: "The idea that your worth is determined by you is about as far from the gospel message as one could travel. . . . As for the proof of our worth, it lies in the fact that God has made us his children and redeemed us."

The Christian faith is also realistic in not ignoring our sin. "Christianity wants you to feel good about yourself, but not until there is something to feel good about. It would like to get us on the road to recovery before it congratulates us on our good health" (Kilpatrick).

Our worth does not depend on our loving ourselves but on the fact that God loved us so much that he was willing to give his Son for us, and to send his Spirit into our hearts. God calls us his children. This is the true source of self-esteem.

 Loving Father, I thank you for calling me your child. Self-love comes and goes; your love for me never wavers.

Today affirm: "I am God's daughter and he loves me."

■ RECEIVING GOD'S THOUGHTS

Isa. 55:6-9:   "For my thoughts are not your thoughts, neither are your ways my ways, declares the Lord" (v. 8).

A mother was tucking her young son into bed. "Have you said your prayers?" she asked. "No," the boy replied. "Why not?" the mother asked. "Because there was nothing I wanted."

We may smile at that story, but children aren't the only ones to treat prayer as primarily a way of getting what they want. God does want us to bring our needs to him in prayer, but prayer is more than that. We come in prayer not to get God to do our will, but to open ourselves to doing his will.

Our time of reflecting on God's Word is a chance to get away from our own words and thoughts to receive God's thoughts, to learn from him.

In prayer we open ourselves "to a transformation of conscience and consciousness with all that can lead to. One's life will never be the same again" (Basil Pennington). Our time of prayer may lead us to see ourselves or others in a new light. We may receive a new insight, or peace of mind, or a call to a specific action.

Sometimes it may seem that we receive nothing from our time of prayer. That's all right too. Sometimes it's enough just to be close to God, just because we love him.

 Lord, teach me to pray.

In your prayer, could you be more open and undemanding, willing to let God change you?

■ THE TRANSFORMING FRIENDSHIP

2 Cor. 5:16-21:   "Therefore, if anyone is in Christ, he is a new creation; the old has gone, the new has come!" (v. 17).

Two friends asked me to sing in a trio with them. I was glad I'd be singing more, but even happier that I'd be spending time with these two people. The people we choose to spend time with help determine the kind of person we are becoming. They love us, confront us, and help us do things we never thought we could.

While he was on earth, Jesus changed people's lives by being their friend. A shady tax collector became St. Matthew, and a quick-tempered fisherman became St. Peter. They were still themselves, but they were capable of saying and doing things that were quite beyond them until they became his friends.

The heart of the Christian faith is that we too can know Jesus, and our friendship with him can change our lives. Leslie Weatherhead wrote: "Unless the Church in all its branches is sadly mistaken, unless the saints were deluded, unless the lives of the world's purest and best are based on illusion, that friendship is still available . . . a friendship capable of making us what we most want to be."

 Jesus, my life has been warmed and lighted by your friendship. I thank you.

In what ways is your friendship with Jesus making a difference in your life?

■ LIVING AT PEACE

Rom. 12:14-21: "Do not repay anyone evil for evil. Be careful to do what is right in the eyes of everybody. If it is possible, as far as it depends on you, live at peace with everyone" (vv. 17-18).

Pat agreed to serve as vice-president of the PTA, but as the year went on, she found herself more and more at odds with the president, Alice. To Pat, it seemed that Alice's authoritarian tactics were alienating members and diminishing the effectiveness of the organization, but when she suggested this to Alice, she got nowhere. Finally Pat resigned. But she did it by sending a letter to Alice, explaining her reasons and saying that she loved Alice too much to keep silent.

Alice responded to the letter by calling several other officers of the PTA. She learned that they agreed with Pat. As a result, Alice called Pat, thanking her for the letter, telling her that she wanted to change, and asking Pat to reconsider her resignation.

Pat could have left silently, in a huff. From then on Alice would probably have been her enemy. Because she cared enough to confront Alice, a potential enemy became a better friend.

 Lord, in a conflict, help me avoid the easy way out. Give me the courage and love I need.

Is there any conflict in your life in which you need to run the risk of confrontation for the sake of genuine peace?

■ RIGHTS OR SERVICE?

Matt. 5:38-42: "Give to the one who asks you" (v. 42).

Diane stood with her hands on her hips. "I've had it! No one is going to take advantage of me again—not at home, not at work, not at church. From now on I'm standing up for my rights!"

Jesus never talked about *rights*. In his Sermon on the Mount he even said that we should allow people to take advantage of us! We are not to seek revenge. We should be willing to go the extra mile.

This goes against the grain with us. It is not "natural." Human nature—and our society—says, "Keep accounts. Be sure you get your fair share. Protect your rights." Jesus puts the emphasis elsewhere—not on rights, but on service.

Does this mean that we are to be doormats, at the mercy of everyone's whims? Not at all. The test is the ultimate good of everyone involved. Sometimes to help our children (or our husbands!), we have to tell them, "I won't do that for you. You'll have to learn to do it yourself." Sometimes for the sake of our own physical or mental health, we have to say to some organization, "No, I don't have the time or energy to do that now." But in following Christ, we don't see issues in terms of *rights*, but in terms of what is best for all involved, including ourselves.

 Lord, give me flexibility, so I know when it's best to say yes to people and when I need to say no.

Are there any ways you feel you are being taken advantage of? Are you doing it willingly for the sake of Christ and the benefit of others?

■ PEACEMAKERS

Matt. 5:3-12: "Happy are those who work for peace; God will call them his children" (v. 9 TEV).

Polls show that women, more than men, are inclined to vote for a candidate whose policies seem to promote peace. Many women are concerned enough to take seriously the God-given role of peacemaker. Yet when we see the buildup of arms by governments dominated by men, we may feel powerless to do anything that can make a difference. But, as Dorothy Day, who devoted her life to peace and to helping the poor, said, "No one has a right to sit down and feel hopeless. There's too much work to do."

The actions you choose will depend on your personality and your situation in life. A first step is always to be informed—for example, to read a good book on Russia or China or the issues of disarmament. You may find it helpful to be part of a local group that works for peace. Some women write letters to politicians; others campaign for candidates they believe will promote peace. The point is to do *something*.

Alvin Rogness counters our complacency: "With pious resignation I may say, 'Heaven is my home,' and if the earth blows itself up, I have a dwelling place, eternal, not made with hands. But the earth is the Lord's and we've been given management of it, and until he himself decides to usher in a new one, we can't give it up. So we pray, we hope, and we give whatever support we can to every effort for peace."

 Heavenly Father, as your child, I want to be a peacemaker.

If you have not already, choose one thing you can do for world peace.

■ GIFTS DIFFERING

Rom. 12:3-8: "We have different gifts, according to the grace given us" (v. 6).

For a long time I felt that all my friends were serving God better than I was. One worked hard to improve the public schools. Another was a foster mother for disturbed teenagers. A third was active in her political party. I was sure that being a good Christian meant being like them—only I knew I wasn't, and worse yet, I didn't want to be.

Then we went to Madagascar so my husband could teach English. When we got off the plane, the principal said, "By the way, there's no one to teach music to the elementary and junior high school students. Would you be able to help?" I agreed to try, and the more I did it, the better it went.

I began to realize that I had spent years trying to serve God by using gifts I didn't have. Now that one of my gifts had been discovered and put to use, the energy I had spent feeling inadequate could be used to serve others. I worked hard, not only without resentment, but with joy. I could respect others and be grateful that they had gifts that were different from mine and so could accomplish things that I could not. I could accept my part in the body of Christ, knowing that I was a valuable member with something to give. Best of all, by identifying my gifts I could get my thoughts off myself and onto the needs of others.

 Lord, I thank you for the unique gifts you have given me. Help me identify them, rejoice in them, and use them for the benefit of others.

Make a list of your gifts and talents. Ask others to help you recognize your gifts.

■ GROWTH THROUGH DISCIPLINE

James 4:8: "Come near to God and he will come near to you."

Many of us are discovering that Christian growth does not happen apart from some disciplines like spiritual reading, meditation, prayer, journaling, Bible study, and worship. Henri Nouwen has said that discipleship can never be real without discipline.

Many of us—I was one—rebel against the idea of self-discipline. It seems easier to do "what comes naturally." But I've found that neglect of spiritual disciplines leads only to stagnation and frustration.

Disciplines make the time and space in which God can affect our lives. He is always with us, but only through discipline can we become quiet enough to recognize his presence, to hear his voice from among the many that speak to us. Someone has called this "active passivity." We grow by receiving, but we have to do certain things in order to receive. God is eager to give; our task is to learn and practice those disciplines by which we receive.

I don't do the disciplines in order to win God's approval; I know I already have that. I don't even do them to feel I've made a certain amount of "progress" or to "make" growth happen. I just do them, and leave the results to God.

 Lord, I desire to grow in grace. Help me be faithful to the disciplines by which I can receive.

Read a book on spiritual disciplines like Richard Foster's *Celebration of Discipline*.

■ MAKING CHOICES

Phil. 1:19-26:   "Yet what shall I choose? I do not know!" (v. 22).

Shall I go back to work? Should I get married so soon? Should we have children? What career would be best for me? Should I stay with a stressful relationship? How should I spend this vacation? What kind of life-style do I really want?

We like the freedom to choose, yet it can feel like a burden, especially when we're not sure about our choices.

The apostle Paul felt that tension too. He wanted to leave this life in order to be more fully with Christ, yet he felt he was needed by the young Christians.

It would be easier if God always told us exactly what we are to do, but he doesn't. He gives us the freedom, as mature adults, to make our own choices.

Sometimes we can wait until we sense God's leading. Often the counsel of friends, family, or books will help us clarify our thinking. But sometimes circumstances force us to decide, even when we're not ready. Then we remember that God forgives us our wrong choices! He can redeem our mistakes and get us where he wants us to be in spite of them. If we have to make a decision and get moving, God can correct our course as we go.

 Lord, I'm grateful for the freedom to make choices. I trust in your guidance and your forgiveness.

What are some decisions you have to make right now? Can you wait, or do you have to make a choice?

21

■ GROWING IN LOVE

Ezek. 36:24-28: "I will give you a new heart and put a new spirit in you; I will remove from you your heart of stone and give you a heart of flesh" (v. 26).

A neighbor told me that she was feeling really guilty because she was having a hard time loving one of her children. Many of us have felt this way at some time—about a relative, someone at work or at church, or a difficult child. We say to ourselves, "I must have a heart of stone, God won't forgive me until I shape up, what a terrible person I must be." When we feel unable to love someone, what can we do?

It helps to remind ourselves that God has many resources. *He* loves that person you're having a hard time loving, and he can reach them through other people besides you. Pray for this to happen.

Affirm that you are *becoming* able to love them. Instead of concentrating on your inability to love, concentrate on your ability to change. Tell yourself, whenever you think of the person, that you are slowly becoming able to love him or her. The desire to love is a sign that God is already at work in you.

Above all, relax. Don't try too hard. Constant self-scrutiny is paralyzing. Show love in any small way you can, and trust that God will use that small step to open the way for love to grow.

 Dear Lord, I know I can't produce love. I've tried. But you can. Help me grow in love for _____.

Imagine a small expression of love you can offer. Try it. Reflect on what happens. Can you imagine another small step?

■ COPING WITH CRITICISM

Luke 6:27-36: "Bless those who curse you, pray for those who mistreat you" (v. 28).

W ell, *you* may eat that, but *I* don't give my family junk food."

"Do you realize that your dandelion seeds are blowing into my lawn?"

"If we expect to have decent schools, people like you are going to have to help!"

We all get criticized. What is the best way to react? You may decide the person is wrong—the food you serve your family is nutritious. Maybe she's right—you should hire someone to pull the dandelions. Or you may realize the critic doesn't understand you.

The only way to weather criticism gracefully is to have an inner strength, a clear sense of who we are and why we do what we do. Then we can decide, without being threatened and upset, if someone is right, wrong, or just a different personality than we are. The important thing is not to turn away from those who criticize us, to seek revenge, or to hold a grudge that can poison our own spirit. God's love for us and our own inner strength enable us to react in a healthy way to those who do not agree with us—trying to understand them, wishing them well, and praying for them.

 Lord, I pray for _____ who has criticized me. Help me to know how I should react in this situation.

Has your relationship with someone been hurt because they criticized you? Is there something you can do about it now?

■ FACING FEARS

Isa. 43:1-7: "Fear not, for I have redeemed you; I have called you by name; you are mine" (v. 1).

Fear has a tight grasp. Fear of being unloved. Fear of letting people know what we really think. Fear of commitment. Fear of failure. Fear of the future. Fear of conflict. In the midst of our fears, we hear God's comforting voice: "Fear not. You are mine."

Relying on his promise, you can counter fear.

1. Don't carry your past around with you. What happened before doesn't have to happen again.

2. Express your fears to other people, write them in a journal, talk about them to God.

3. Ask yourself, "What's the worst thing that could happen in this situation?" This can help restore perspective.

4. Find ways to stay aware of God's care and his promises of faithfulness.

5. If you are afraid of something in the future, give yourself some positive experience to look forward to.

6. Use your imagination to picture yourself acting in a calm and relaxed way, free from fear.

7. Become part of a support group. Other people may face the same fears.

8. Take action. Have courage and do something to move toward your goals, trusting in God's supporting presence.

 I will not be afraid or discouraged, O God, because I am yours.

Memorize today's verse. Repeat it when you become fearful.

■ TRUE HUMILITY

Rom. 12:3-8: "Do not think of yourself more highly than you ought, but rather think of yourself with sober judgment, in accordance with the measure of faith God has given you" (v. 3).

Psychologists tell us how important it is that we achieve a high measure of self-esteem. The Christian faith traditionally has emphasized humility. Is there a conflict between these two? Paul tells us not to think more *highly* of ourselves than we ought, but this implies that we should not think more *lowly* of ourselves either.

A false humility can be an easy way out. If I put myself down, I need not risk failure or put forth any effort. I can play it safe: "Oh, I'm not good at that; someone else will do it better."

True humility means taking an honest look not only at my limitations and weaknesses, but also at the strengths God has given me.

I'm helped to do this by being part of Christ's body, where there are many members, each with his or her own function. Knowing this, I don't have to exaggerate my strengths or claim gifts I don't have. I can count on others who have the gifts I don't. But I should not undervalue myself, because my true self-esteem comes from knowing that my unique gifts are as necessary to the body of Christ as anyone else's.

 Lord, I thank you for making me a member of your body. Give me a true perspective on my strengths and weaknesses.

Do you ever give yourself negative nicknames? If so, right now give yourself some affectionate names.

■ GROWING OLD

Ps. 71:1-18:   "Even when I am old and gray, do not
forsake me, O God, till I declare your power to the
next generation, your might to all who are to come"
(v. 18).

Few women look forward to growing old. It fills us
with questions. How will I feel about looking gray and
wrinkled? Will my husband and my friends die a long
time before I do? Will I be lonely? What about my
financial needs?

The day-to-day lives of the aged are unfamiliar to
many of us. It would help us to get to know some
older women, especially those who are coping well
with the process of aging. I picture my friend
Catharine in her beautifully decorated apartment. The
whole retirement center has a pleasant atmosphere
offering a full range of activities to keep mind and
body healthy. Catharine at age 80 is still reading,
attending and leading Bible studies, and continuing
her career as a free-lance writer. She makes me feel a
lot better about growing older.

Catharine wrote in one of her books, "The longer I
live, the more the prayers of elderly children of God
impress me. Instead of asking for material blessings,
they sing praise to God. Instead of trusting in human
strength, they rely on the Savior and joyfully thank
him for the power of the Holy Spirit."

 "Thou will support us both when little and even
to gray hairs" (St. Augustine).

Are you a close friend of at least one older woman?

■ UNCONDITIONAL LOVE

Jer. 31:3-6: "I have loved you with an everlasting love; I have drawn you with loving-kindness" (v. 3).

I sit, coffee cup in hand, across the table from my friend Joan, and it suddenly becomes very real to me—"She *does* like me, in spite of all my shortcomings."

My youngest child gives me a peanut buttery hug and says, "I love you mommy."

My husband brings me a cup of coffee in bed and gets the children off to school by himself.

Experiences like these help me understand the unconditional love of God.

A retreat leader said, "The beginning of all spirituality is that I *admit* God's unconditional love for me"—that I accept God's love, not just on an intellectual level, but in my deepest, innermost being. I admit it, that is, I let it in.

It's hard for us to avoid the feeling that we have to earn God's love, that he must be disappointed in us as we are, because we so often fall short. But, thanks be to God, he doesn't wait to love me until I'm good enough. He loves me right now.

Joan taught me to pray one of the best and shortest prayers I've ever heard: "God, here I am, as I am."

 God, here I am, as I am.

Put your name into the Bible verse: "_____, I have loved you with an everlasting love."

27

■ JOY

Isa. 61:7:   "Your joy will last forever" (TEV).

It's easy to begin feeling that life for women is difficult—lots of problems to be solved, choices to be made, work to do—that only a humorless, determined attitude will get the job done. What a grim way to live!

What about "I have told you this so that my joy may be in you and that your joy may be complete" (John 15:11) and "The fruit of the Spirit is love, joy . . ." (Gal. 5:22)? God means for us to be filled with joy. He does so many things every day to bring us joy. It's we who keep the joy locked in and buried because we are so busy concentrating on what we don't have instead of what we do have.

Gratitude is the surest way to release the joy that is in all of us. The more we give thanks to God, right where we are, right when we think of it, the more joyful we will become. Start with the little things—a sunny day, a compliment from a friend, a car that runs. Move on to the bigger things. "Thanks that I'm healthy enough to *do* all this work. Thanks that there *are* choices. Thanks that there is someone to *help* me with this problem."

There are lots of reasons to feel great about being a woman, and lots of reasons to feel great about being alive. Rejoice in the Lord always!

 Lord, you have done great things for us; we are glad.

On a piece of paper or in your journal, begin to make a list of all that you have to be grateful for, now and in your past.

■ LOVE, HONOR, AND OBEY

John 14:15-31: "If you love me, you will obey what I command" (v. 15).

Obedience is not a popular word today. It is left out of marriage vows, because women are unwilling to give someone power over their lives, even a man they love. Yet in our relationship with God, obedience is the only way to our own highest good. In the life of Jesus, we see what it really means.

Henri Nouwen explains: "The word obedience has many negative connotations in our society. It makes us think of authority figures who impose their wills against our desires. It makes us remember unhappy childhood events, or hard tasks performed under threats of punishment. But none of this applies to Jesus' obedience. His obedience means a total fearless listening to his loving Father. Between the Father and the Son there is only love."

Obedience to God is not submission to a heartless tyrant. When we know we are loved, and when we love in return, we *want* to please the other person. That relationship becomes more precious than anything—or anyone—else. That is what Jesus is talking about when he says "If anyone loves me, he will obey my teaching. My Father will love him, and we will come to him and make our home with him" (John 14:23). As our love for God grows, he changes our hearts, so that we "delight in his will and walk in his ways."

 God, when I remember that your central concern is my welfare, it's easier to obey.

What is your attitude toward obedience—to other people—to God?

■ GIVE SOLITUDE

Mark 1:35: "Jesus got up, left the house and went off to a solitary place, where he prayed."

At a Christian camp where I was a canoe guide, each 10-day trip included a "solitude day." In the morning, the campers were dropped off on islands or points of land out of sight and hearing of any other camper. Each had a lunch, Bible, paper, and pencil. As I picked them up, one by one, in the evening, the girls would often tell me that this was the first day they had ever spent alone. It was almost invariably a high point of their trip.

What did they like so much about being alone? Being quiet. The freedom from being what someone else expected. The freedom to plan their own day or not to plan at all. The freedom to pray in any way they wished—even to talk out loud to God. The time to discover some things about themselves. The feeling of closeness to God out there in the wilderness.

Solitude is a gift we could give more often to those we love, and to ourselves. To our children solitude is a whole day in which no one will disturb them. To a husband solitude is a day, or even a week, to go away alone without feeling guilty for not being with the family. To a friend solitude is a retreat as a gift. To the mother of small children solitude is free daycare so she can get away. To ourselves solitude is a change in our busy schedule so that there is time to be quiet and alone.

 Lord, help me not to have solitude always at the bottom of my "things to do" list.

Think of one person to whom you would like to give a gift of solitude. Arrange to do so as soon as possible.

■ FRIENDS

Rom. 16:1-6:   "She has been a great help to many people, including me" (v. 2).

Paul is sometimes accused of disparaging females, yet he counted among his closest friends many women. In his letter to the Romans he mentions Prisca and her husband Aquila, and Mary, a hard worker in the church there. He especially commended Phoebe, who helped many, including Paul himself. Paul needed friends (male and female), and we do too.

I have found that I need a variety of friends—old and young, male and female, single and married, some like me and some very different. God has brought into my life some people I would never have chosen, yet they have proved very important to me. The greater the variety of my friends, the more my life is enriched.

I need friends who are near. In our transient society relatives and friends are often far away, but I also need a friend close by to whom I can go when I can't manage my troubles by myself. I need friends who accept me as I am and who make me feel good about myself, but who will also challenge me when I'm off base. I need friends who share my spiritual journey, who understand the way I am trying to live and share the same goals and questions. I need friends who celebrate my joys and successes with me.

And I've learned that in order to have friends like this I need to be this kind of friend.

Dear God, lead me to the people I need and the people who need me.

What do you look for in a friend? Who are the friends with whom you can really share your life? Today give thanks for them.

■ STORING UP TREASURES

Matt. 6:19-34:   "Where your treasure is, there your heart will be also" (v. 21).

Recently my friend Helen shared the conflict she feels over their possessions. "The way we buy, eat, and relate to others isn't what it should be. But because of where I am, I feel locked into a way of living that's not what God wants for me. And as our kids get older, they want to conform even more. I get so tired of struggling with them I just give in."

Probably many of us share this feeling. We know there's a big gap between Jesus' words and the way we live, but we find it hard to resist the pressures of our consumer-oriented society. And our feelings are very mixed. Because we're created with a love of beauty, most of us prefer attractive surroundings, and that usually costs money. And we enjoy having money to give where *we* think it's needed.

So often women are the ones who make the majority of the decisions about household spending. It would be easier if God gave us clear rules. But God has left the decisions to us.

The only way I've found for dealing with these choices is to stay in close fellowship with other Christians who can help my decision making, to be grateful for all the possessions I do have, and to give away or share as much as we possibly can.

 Lord, I thank you for all your good gifts. Help me to remember where my true treasure is and to keep a right perspective on my possessions.

How does your faith influence your finances? Find an opportunity to discuss this with at least one other woman.

■ CHILDREN AT PLAY

Matt. 18:1-4:   "Unless you change and become like little children, you will never enter the kingdom of heaven" (v. 3).

I peeked out the window and saw the children dressed in costumes—old scarves, gaudy jewelry, colorful long skirts. "You be the princess and I'll be the old witch." For hours they were completely lost in their play, oblivious to everything around them.

When's the last time you lost yourself in play? Many of us don't play very much, and even when we try to have fun we're so self-conscious and inhibited that we can't really let go.

When Jesus said that we should become like children, maybe part of what he meant is that we need to learn to play again, in the easy spontaneous way of a child.

To do that, we may have to consider some new form of recreation—a new sport, a game, a handcraft, or joining a musical or theatre group. And we may have to run the risk of looking a little foolish.

At age 38 I started tap dancing and aerobics. I still feel silly, but I'm having a wonderful time. My body no longer feels like a useless appendage to my head.

In family life, work, and religion we can become overburdened by "shoulds, oughts, and musts." By learning to play again, we revive our spirits and air out our stuffy souls.

 Lord, let me dare to play again like a child.

What are the ways you play? Be open to trying something new.

◼ LEARNING COMPASSION

Rom. 12:15: "Rejoice with those who rejoice; mourn with those who mourn."

Awakened one morning by the sound of sirens, I looked out the window and saw the rescue squad next door. Within minutes, a paramedic was at my door saying, "Your neighbor's husband just passed away. She's asked for you until her relatives come." I went, wondering, "What good will I do? What can I say?" I didn't say much of anything, just sat there with my arms around her.

Compassion is to suffer, to be in pain with someone else. Jesus showed compassion when he wept for Lazarus, fed the hungry, healed the sick. For us, compassion sometimes comes hard, because we want to avoid pain and struggle, to pretend it's not even there if we can. How does one begin to learn compassion?

We can try to overcome the feeling that we must *do* something. It's often enough just to go, spend time, stay without running away. We can make the time we spend good time. We so instinctively apologize—"I wish I could do more." Just to be *all* there while we *are* there, giving our full attention and our love—that is what matters. And, as Henri Nouwen says, when we leave, God stays.

 Lord, keep me from being afraid when someone needs me. Help me write, or call, or go be with them. Help me think about *them,* and not about what I will say or do.

Think of one person you have avoided because of their pain. Make some contact with that person.

■ RECEIVING GUESTS

Gen. 18:1-15: "When he saw them, he hurried from the entrance of his tent to meet them . . . . Do not pass your servant by . . . let me get you something to eat, so you can be refreshed and then go on your way" (vv. 2, 3, 5).

During our four years in Madagascar we enjoyed the warm and gracious hospitality of several missionary families. Because they were busy people, they went about their work and let us join in as we wished. At mealtime everyone gathered for good food and good conversation.

This experience made me think about myself as a hostess. While I wanted guests, I didn't always enjoy the additional pressure. I wondered if people really felt welcome in our home.

Since learning from these families what hospitality means, we've enjoyed our guests much more. I still get done what I have to, but I'm more flexible. I know now that gourmet meals aren't necessary; just sharing what we have is enough.

 Thank you, Lord, for those who have shown me what it is to be welcomed. Help me pay attention to those who come to my home.

The next time you hesitate to invite guests because what you have to offer won't be "good enough," go ahead and invite them anyway!

■ HOW LONG, O LORD?

Lam. 3:1-33: "Let him bury his face in the dust—
there may yet be hope" (v. 29).

A teenager rebels and wastes his life on alcohol and
drugs. A marriage goes through years of painful
struggle. An aging parent suffers disability and pain.
Some problems go on for so long and seem so hopeless
that we can hardly bear to ask God for help anymore.

We may never be able to answer that question: why
does God allow such bad things to happen to us? But
we begin to realize that we can learn and grow
through them. A seed sprouts always in the darkness
of the earth, and much spiritual growth begins in the
darkness of pain, loss, sickness, and disappointment.
In this life suffering will never be eliminated, but we
believe that God can work in all things for our good.
(Rom. 8:28).

"Faith sometimes falters, because he does not
reward us immediately," wrote St. Augustine. "But
hold out, be steadfast, bear the delay, and you have
carried the cross." God is never a God of
hopelessness. We dare to keep asking for changes in
situations that look hopeless. Even if God does not
change the situation, he can change us. This is most
certainly true.

 Lord, I trust in you; so great is your unfailing
love.

**Think of a friend who is facing a long-term problem.
Send a card or letter, including Lam. 3:25-26.**

36

■ CHERISH THE GIFTS

Ps. 116:12-19: "I will sacrifice a thank offering to you and call on the name of the Lord" (v. 17).

Along with most of my friends I used to complain about grocery shopping. "Everything is so expensive! Hauling those heavy bags through the snowdrifts is such a hassle. Why does the store have to be jammed just when I go?"

Then we went as missionaries to Madagascar for four years. The shelves in the tiny stores were often empty. The market provided good food but few choices. When we returned to the United States, I pushed my cart down the supermarket aisles with a grateful heart.

Although my perspective was radically altered, I was aware that it wasn't my job to start telling everybody how grateful they should be. But I do know that for me, gratitude has made my life much happier. It has also acted as a magnet for blessings: the more grateful I've become, the more I've had to be grateful for.

An ancient prayer expresses this thanks: "Blessed art thou, O Lord, who givest us this bread and this wine, the fruit of man's labor." This prayer recognizes that our blessings depend in part on our labor: we shape ourselves, our world, and our history. But all, finally, is a gift of God, and we ourselves are the finest of his gifts. Our gift to God is our gratitude.

 Lord, help us to cherish the gifts that surround us, to share your blessings, and to live in joyful gratitude.

Imagine that everything and everyone around you has a little tag on it that says, "To _____ , from God." What special gift is yours today?

■ BORN FREE

Gal. 5:1: "It is for freedom that Christ has set us free."

Maria wanted to be free of all the old ways—free of her parents, free of her church, free from moral standards, free to "do her own thing." Her quest for freedom led her straight into slavery—slavery to an emotional roller coaster, slavery to the men whose beds she shared.

Psychologist Erich Fromm wrote a book entitled *Escape from Freedom*. He says that while many people think they want freedom, they find it too difficult, and so escape into various forms of unfreedom. One way to escape is to obey rules. Women are seeking to be liberated from some of the old rules like "Thou shalt be docile and submissive," "Thou shalt not work outside the home," and "Thou shalt have a perfectly clean house." But in the process, it's easy to fall into a new set of rules, rules like "Thou shalt not be just a housewife," "Thou shalt wear blue jeans," and "Thou shalt not refer to God as 'He'."

Either way, life under laws is a form of bondage. Paul says that Jesus came to free us from a life under bondage to law for a life of loving service. Knowing we are the free daughters of God, we can resist both the old laws and the new. We can make our own decisions, with the guidance of God's Spirit.

 Lord, I thank you that I am not bound by old rules and old limitations, or by new rules and new limitations, but am free in you.

Make a list of "rules" of our society that you usually follow.

■ PRAY CONTINUALLY

1 Thess. 5:16-18: "Pray continually" (v. 17).

It's easy to roll over and snuggle under those covers for a few more minutes in the morning. When I do that, my day often feels different than if I take some time for prayer.

Jesus' life clearly shows that we need to make these special times for quiet prayer and that morning is one of the best. But we can't always put off praying until that time comes. We can get used to praying whatever we're doing—peeling vegetables, driving on the freeway, shopping, waiting in line. We don't have to wait until our work is done in order to pray. "Accustom yourself gradually to carry prayer into all your daily occupations. Speak, move, work in peace, as if you were in prayer" (Francois Fenelon).

The prayers don't have to be long or carefully worded. We should pray in whatever way we find easiest.

When I begin to worry, I can just say, "God, I leave this with you." When I'm grateful, "Thank you for my house, for the light shining in the window." When I remember my friend, "Lord, bless him, and may your will be done in his life." When I'm awake in the middle of the night, I often get back to sleep by praying for relatives and friends.

If we pray these short prayers every time we think of it, they soon become second nature.

 Lord, help me find times of quiet and solitude, but remind me to pray always.

Whenever you think *about* prayer, *pray*, if only for a moment.

■ THE EXTENDED CHURCH

Matt. 18:20:   "For where two or three come together in my name, there am I with them."

One local church may have a strong Bible study program. Another specializes in music. Still another may have an active ministry to the needy. It's a rare church that can do everything well. So we may find that our local congregation is meeting some of our needs, but not all.

For a time I felt frustrated by that. Then a friend introduced me to the concept of the "extended church." We've learned that the nuclear family of husband, wife, and children can't be everything to us. We need an extended family of relatives and friends. In the same way we don't have to demand that our local church meet all of our spiritual needs. Because God wants us to grow spiritually, he has many resources for allowing that to happen.

My "extended church" includes Christian friends of all kinds. Someone has called this a "network of the heart": people joined together because they care about one another and share the same spiritual journey. My extended church includes a retreat house where I go from time to time seeking solitude and prayer, spiritual writers throughout the world whose ideas and experiences have helped me, and friends from other churches who give me a perspective on the faith I would not otherwise have.

 I thank you, Lord, for all the ways you come to me with your grace and power.

What is included in your "extended church"?

■ LEAVE YOURSELF ALONE

Psalm 139:   "O Lord, you have searched me and you know me" (v. 1).

I cheered when I saw the title of Eugenia Price's book: *Leave Yourself Alone: Set Yourself Free from the Paralysis of Analysis.* If I could just forget about myself for a while! What a relief!

The self-help and self-development focus has helped many of us make positive changes in our lives. But it can also cause us to become involved in endless analyzing, comparing ourselves with "experts," or beginning self-improvement schemes that always fall short of our expectations.

We do need to know ourselves, but, Eugenia Price asks, "What do we do with our messy selves once we know them?" Until I believe that God will save me, I keep trying to save myself. Sometimes my job is to get out of the way and let God work on me. But how? Eugenia Price says, "The healthy-minded person is one who is focused most often, not on herself, but on God and other people." It is in seeking a personal relationship with God and with other people that my life is renewed and my true self is revealed.

C. S. Lewis put it this way: "Your real, new self (which is Christ's and also yours just because it is his) will not come as long as you are looking for it. It will come when you are looking for him."

 God, you know me better than I do. You care about me more than I can. I can leave myself alone because I know you won't.

Is there some area of your life that you have spent too much energy analyzing? Can you let go of it for a while and reach outward to someone else?

■ TRUSTING THE WORD

Isa. 55:6-11: "[My word] will not return to me empty, but will accomplish what I desire and achieve the purpose for which I sent it" (v. 11).

My grandmother was a great pack rat. She squirreled away string, magazines, paper, and other odds and ends, because "You'll never know when you'll need this." Something like this can happen in regard to our use of God's Word. After a friend of ours lost a son in an automobile accident, he said, "In order to handle this, I needed all the Bible study and prayer I had ever done."

Sometimes my Bible study or spiritual reading speaks directly to the questions I'm asking. At other times it seems to have little connection with my life. But then later, even years later, an experience causes me to remember something I heard in a sermon or read in a book. Suddenly that truth becomes real for me. I begin to live the truth—but only as I need it.

Realizing this, I take a more relaxed attitude toward my spiritual reading, churchgoing, and studying. Those truths I can't use now will be available to me when I need them. God's Word will bear fruit at the right time.

Jesus said, "All this I have spoken while still with you. But the Counselor, the Holy Spirit, whom the Father will send in my name, will teach you all things and remind you of everything I have said to you" (John 14:25-26).

 Lord, I thank you for the gift of your Word. I pray that it will always accomplish in my life what you want.

Have you ever experienced an old truth coming alive for you in the midst of a new experience?

■ OF TIMES AND SEASONS

Eccles. 3:1-8: "There is a time for everything, and a season for every activity under heaven" (v. 1).

In the 'summer' of life, we experience exhilaration, openness, the freedom to challenge and be challenged. In 'autumns' we suffer a loss, or stripping of vitality. In the 'springs' we know the wholeness and growth of peace and joy. Before this time of newness and growth, there was 'winter'—a period of defeat, or a time of struggling and suffering" (Susan Muto).

Our lives are made of seasons like these. I may like some better than others, but I'm learning to accept each as it comes. I'm trying not to miss any season, but to experience each one and to sense the movements from one to another without trying to prolong any season beyond its intended span. Each season has its own character and beauty.

When a particular season passes, I may feel sad or relieved, but I do not need to feel fearful. I can see the next stage as one in which to grow and learn. If I can let go of the tasks and problems—and even the joys—of the old season, I am open to receive new joys, new opportunities for creativity and life.

 My times are in your hands, O Lord.

What "season" is it in your life right now? Is there anything you need to let go of to prepare the way for the new season?

■ HELP OF THE HELPLESS

Rom. 7:15-25: "What a wretched man I am! Who will rescue me from this body of death? Thanks be to God—through Jesus Christ our Lord!" (vv. 24-25).

As a child, I enjoyed Uncle Remus's story of Brer Rabbit and the Tar Baby, and now I enjoy reading it to my children. They laugh when the rabbit gets stuck, and the more he struggles the stucker he gets.

This is not just a funny story; it's a parable of our lives. We get stuck—and how often it seems the harder we struggle, the worse things get. How true are Paul's words: "I do not understand what I do. For what I want to do I do not do, but what I hate I do" (Rom. 7:15). We too feel "wretched" and wonder how we can ever change.

We can find deliverance in the same place that Paul did. "Thanks be to God—through Jesus Christ our Lord." God can deliver us from our self-centered striving, if in the midst of our struggle we turn to him for strength and peace and freedom. Like Paul, we will probably continue to experience the battle within. There is no guarantee of instant victory. But we know that the Holy Spirit is at work in our lives—through the Word, through prayer and worship, through Christian friends and counselors. Like Paul, we can also say, "Thanks be to God!"

 Lord, sometimes I get discouraged because there's such a gap between what I am and what I want to be. I trust in you for forgiveness, and I look to you for deliverance.

What is the biggest "stuck" area in your life? Believe God can free you. Expect something to happen.

■ LONG-DISTANCE FRIENDS

I Thess. 2:17-3:13: "How can we thank God enough for you in return for all the joy we have in the presence of our God because of you?" (3:9).

In a society where one-fifth of all families move every year, we often become separated from our most precious friends. The apostle Paul experienced that too, and mentions it often in his letters. His words touch on many of our feelings for our separated friends: our good memories of them, our gratitude, the pain of separation, the joy of sending and receiving news, the longing to see them again, the promise to pray for one another.

Good friends are one of God's best gifts, and such friendships are worth the effort it takes to nourish them and keep them alive. There are many ways to do this. We can revive the gentle art of letter writing. We can make use of the telephone or send tapes. Sometimes we can go a bit out of our way on a trip and stop for a visit. We can send an occasional book or magazine article that has meant something to us. Through prayer we can be together in the presence of God even though we are separated on earth.

Novelist George Eliot wrote: "Those children of God whom it has been given to have communion together can never be sundered though the hills should lie between, for they bear one another about in their thoughts continually, as it were a new strength."

 Lord, I thank you for those precious friends who now live far away. I know that your presence is with us and bridges the distance.

This week, do something to reach out to one distant friend.

■ LIFE WITH MOTHER

Deut. 5:16: "Honor your father and your
mother. . .so that you may live long. . . ."

A recent psychological study determined that people
who have developed harmonious relationships with
their parents are happier and live longer than those
who have not—which is exactly what God promised!

Accepting who I am means, in part, accepting my
mother—who she has been and who she is. For many
women, a welcome change in their relationship with
their mothers comes around age 35. Before this, our
main question is "How does she affect me?" After this,
the questions become more "Who is she? How does
she feel? Why does she think and act the way she
does?" We go from demanding that our mothers
understand us to trying to understand what life has
been like for them. It becomes easier to forgive things
we may have resented and appreciate strengths we
didn't recognize before.

For example, I've known for years that my mother's
house burned down and her mother died the year she
was four; that she had a genuine "wicked stepmother,"
and that she ran away from home at 16. But only in
the last few years have I really thought about how that
might have affected her.

As we mature, we can begin to experience the joy of
getting to know our mothers as separate people, with
their own thoughts, feelings, and problems. This is
true "honor." Not the obedience of a child, but the
mutual respect and sharing of two adults.

 Thank you, God, for my mother, for giving us
to one another. Bless her with a loving
daughter.

**What could you do to get to know your mother
better?**

■ WONDERFULLY MADE

Ps. 139:7-18: "I praise you because I am fearfully and wonderfully made" (v. 14).

Our culture bombards us with messages about fashion, glamour, exercise, nutrition, and care of the body. The Bible stresses inner beauty: "Your beauty should not come from outward adornment, such as braided hair and the wearing of gold jewelry and fine clothes. Instead, it should be that of your inner self, the unfading beauty of a gentle and quiet spirit" (1 Peter 3:3-4). This Christian principle is worth stressing again in a society that often measures women by how decorative they are.

Yet we also recognize that our bodies are God's creation, "fearfully and wonderfully made." We know that body, mind, and spirit are closely interrelated. The way I exercise and eat and how I look can make a big difference in how I feel and how I relate to others.

While I do not have to buy into the current obsession with a "beautiful bod," I can make the most of God's work. I like the attitude of Pat's mother, who recently moved to a nursing home at age 86. Pat got her all settled in. A few days later when she came back to visit, her mother appeared with hair combed, a new dress, and lots of makeup—one cheek considerably redder than the other. "You look so nice, mom," Pat said. "Why are you all dressed up?"

"Well," her mother replied, "I don't want to make anyone here feel worse than they already do."

 Lord, "your works are wonderful. I know that full well." You made all creation to be beautiful, including me.

How do you feel about your appearance? Do you want to make any changes?

■ MUCH FROM LITTLE

I Cor. 1:19-31:   "But God chose the foolish things of the world to shame the wise; God chose the weak things of the world to shame the strong" (v. 27).

I always enjoy stories of ordinary people who did something great—like Gladys Aylward, "The Little Woman," a 20-year-old English woman who became a remarkable missionary to China. I love Mother Teresa because of the utter simplicity with which she began one of the greatest ministries of our time. These are ordinary women doing the extraordinary, surprising even themselves.

God does that—uses the small and insignificant to accomplish great things. He took an old couple, Abraham and Sarah, and made a great nation of Israel. He took the few loaves and fishes of a small boy and fed 5000. He used a tiny baby to redeem the world.

Sometimes we feel we don't have much to offer. Others have a better education, more money, greater leadership ability. But if we give God what we have, he can do more than we expect. What's one thing we always have to give? Ourselves. Nothing more, nothing less.

 Lord, I thank you that being an ordinary person does not prevent my being of use to you.

Do you have some dream that you've always thought you were too ordinary to attempt? Today offer God what you have—yourself—and trust that he will use it to accomplish his will.

■ CARRIED TO JESUS

Luke 5:17-26: "Some men came carrying a paralytic on a mat and tried to take him into the house to lay him before Jesus" (v. 18).

The man was paralyzed, unable to help himself. Luckily for him, he had friends who cared so much for him that they carried his pallet to the house where Jesus was. And when they couldn't get to Jesus because of the crowd, they didn't give up—they carried the man onto the roof, removed the light roof covering, and let the man down right in front of Jesus. And because of *their* faith, Jesus forgave and healed the paralyzed man.

There may be times when we are so tired or sick, so discouraged or depressed that we have the strength to do nothing for ourselves. We too are paralyzed. But Christian friends, by their prayers, will carry us to Jesus. If you've had the experience of knowing friends were praying for you, you know what a gift this is.

It's a gift we can offer to others, too. We may not be able to take part in their healing; their problems may be more than we can handle. But we, by our prayers, carry that person into the presence of God, who will respond to *our* faith by offering healing and forgiveness.

 Lord, I thank you for the friends who have prayed for me. Help me not to forget those who need me to bring them to you.

Think of one friend who needs your prayers. Know that you are bringing this person into the presence of Jesus for healing.

■ LET TOMORROW WORRY

Matt. 6:25-34: "Therefore do not worry about tomorrow, for tomorrow will worry about itself" (v. 34).

My friend Charette said, "I grew up believing that somebody in the family had to worry. Since my husband wouldn't, I would. I figured that when he finally grew up, he'd worry the way I did. Now I realize that he's right, and that I want to become more like him."

Worry is really our inability to trust in God's care, to rest from our exaggerated sense of responsibility. When I worry, I become my own god. O. Hallesby, in his famous book *Prayer*, describes so well how it feels to trust God instead of worrying: "We experience wonderful peace and security by leaving our difficulties, both great and small, with him, who is not only solicitous for our welfare but who also understands what is best for us. . . . We have left the matter in the hands of Jesus, and we can go back to our duties secure and happy. He has taken the matter in hand and is fulfilling our desires. Instead of our former anxiety and worry we shall often be able to experience now a certain child-like inquisitiveness, having left the matter in the hands of Jesus. We shall say to ourselves, 'It will be interesting now to see how he solves this difficulty.' "

Lord, I now lay aside my importance and my busyness. Give me the peace that comes with knowing that my life is in your hands. Take away my worry and give me a quiet mind.

The next time you begin to worry, say to yourself instead, "It will be interesting to see how God is going to solve this."

■ WAITING IN A STRANGE LAND

Jer. 29:4-14: "I alone know the plans I have for you, plans to bring you prosperity and not disaster, plans to bring about the future you hope for" (v. 11 TEV).

I met Jan at a retreat. She was about 30, attractive, with two small children. Several months before, her husband had called her from his office and informed her that he was leaving her to live with his secretary.

A woman abandoned is an exile in a strange land—shocked, abused at the very core of her being, tempted to devastating self-pity. Jan said that her greatest struggle had been to learn to wait. "If I just wait, God can change me. If I jump too soon in some direction that I choose, I'll cheat myself of the time I need to go through this and experience what God has in mind for me."

The children of Israel also lived in exile, captive in a strange land. Jeremiah wrote them a letter assuring them of God's help in the midst of their difficulties. But they had to wait until God was ready to give them the good future he had promised.

God has never promised us that our lives will be free of difficulties, or even of intense pain, but he has promised to remain with us. Others may not be faithful, but God is. He knows our needs and he will meet them. The same God who took care of the Israelites in a strange land will care for us. We go on with life, waiting in faith for God to give us the future we hope for.

 Lord, thank you for caring about my life. Help me to wait in faith for your plans to unfold.

Memorize today's text.

■ HAPPY ARE THOSE

Matt. 5:1-12: "Happy are those whose greatest desire is to do what God requires; God will satisfy them fully!" (v. 6 TEV).

According to Jesus, happy (or blessed) are those who are poor, those who mourn, the pure in heart, the peacemakers. An odd collection.

If you were writing your own list of those who are happy, who would you include? Happy are those who are young and healthy, those with no financial problems, those who are fashionably thin, those women with successful careers?

It's important that we know where true happiness is found, because our vision of happiness will influence how we live. What many Christians have learned through the years is that true lasting happiness comes from loving God and other people and from becoming absorbed in some worthwhile activity.

This is no cheap happiness. Loving other people involves struggle, sacrifice, and self-discipline. But as we forget ourselves and focus on others, we become happy.

About work, Elton Trueblood wrote, "Our happiest moments are not those in which we ask how to be happy, but rather those in which we so lose ourselves in some creative task that we forget to take our own emotional pulse."

To the extent that we quit worrying about whether we're happy, God can give us happiness.

Lord, help me find the people and the work that cause me to lose sight of myself.

What people or what work has brought you happiness in the past year?

■ EMOTIONAL ROLLER COASTER

Psalm 42: "Why are you downcast, O my soul?
Why so disturbed within me? Put your hope in God,
for I will yet praise him, my Savior and my God"
(v. 5).

One of the most exciting moments in my life was
when we met our Vietnamese adopted son, Paul. A
social worker carried him out of the plane and placed
him in my arms. Tears of joy rolled down my face.
Friends, TV cameramen, and five sets of new parents
rejoiced together. We drove home in a state of
ecstasy.

The next morning was gray and overcast. Awakened
too early by a screaming infant, both my husband and
I were depressed and irritable all day. We had
crashed.

The psalm writers knew that kind of emotional roller
coaster too. In Psalm 42 the writer says that tears have
been his food day and night. Then he remembers that
he worshiped at the temple with shouts of joy and
thanksgiving.

Emotions are gifts of God that give sparkle and
flavor to life. They can also be good clues to what is
wrong in our lives. But there are certainly times when
we proceed to do what we must do, despite our
feelings. In the words of George Macdonald, "Heed
not thy feelings. Do thy work."

 Lord, help me feel and express my emotions
but not let them become overly important in my
life.

**Have you noticed times in your life when an
emotional high is followed by a deep low?**

■ JOY AFTER WEEPING

John 16:17-24: "You will grieve, but your grief will turn to joy" (v. 20).

One day I was sitting with a friend, praying with her and crying because I was feeling miserable over the loss of someone I loved. Then something struck us funny, and we started to laugh as hard as we'd been crying. I realized that God was beginning to answer my prayers just by reminding me that I could still laugh.

Freedom from pain often comes through grieving, but for the Christian there is joy even in the midst of grief. Louis Evely wrote: "Christian joy is not an easy contentment, a naive self-satisfaction, or even a naive satisfaction for the sake of others. It is a *sadness overcome.*"

We know that by ourselves we cannot overcome sadness or produce happiness. But "God shows himself, manifests himself, only in achieving the impossible, in showing us that he is capable of making appear in us this impossible thing; his joy in our sadness, his happiness in our poverty, his beatitude in our distress" (Evely).

What a gift! And what a gift to have friends who will both laugh and cry with us. God gives us tears and laughter and friends as we need them. We need only ask. "Ask and you will receive, and your joy will be complete" (v. 24).

 Lord, I thank you that you give us your joy even in the midst of our sadness.

Can you recall a time when God gave you unexpected joy in sadness?

■ THAT THREE-LETTER WORD

Song of Songs 2:3-13: "My lover spoke and said to me, 'Arise, my darling, my beautiful one, and come with me' " (v. 10).

Sex is a gift of God, one of the great joys of life. It can make us feel wonderfully alive, like the beloved in the Song of Songs.

While today we know—at least with our minds—that sex is not wrong or inferior, many of us still find it difficult to talk about. Women will often begin, "I've never said this to anyone" or "I've never talked about this before." We may still be shackled by the idea that Christian women don't have certain feelings.

A certain modesty or reserve on sexual matters is appropriate. No one needs the obscenity or gross joking that characterizes so many TV shows or movies. But at times it is helpful to discuss the joys or problems of sexual life with other women—and with our partners. Single or recently divorced women, for example, may need to talk about their sexual needs and how they can be met in ways that are right for a Christian. Within marriage, too, problems can arise which can severely threaten the marriage. When brought out into the open and discussed, perhaps with a counselor, they can be worked through.

God wants us whole and happy in this part of our life too. God cares about the decisions we make and is willing to help us.

 Lord, thank you for the gift of sexuality. Free me to talk about it in ways that are helpful.

Do you have friends with whom you can talk about sex when you need to?

■ LEARNING BY IMITATION

Phil. 3:17-21: "Join with others in following my example. . . and take note of those who live according to the pattern we gave you" (v. 17).

Because we learn so much by observing others, we need good models of the Christian life. I think of some of the models in my life: Renie, for her enthusiasm and hospitality; Louise, for her thoughtfulness; Terry, for her love of children; Marie, for her prayer.

I'm not just like any of them. But I love to be with them. They don't make me feel inferior; they don't intimidate me. I learn from them and yet feel perfectly happy to be myself.

I think this is because they are simply *themselves*. They don't imply that anyone should be like them. They think I'm fine the way I am. Occasionally, in a gentle way, they tell me something I need to hear.

In our circle of personal acquaintances, we may not have all the models we need. But as part of the great Christian family, we have a vast array of examples to imitate. There are the great men and women of the Bible. There are the great saints and humanitarians, past and present, from whom we learn by reading their stories. All of them give us new vision, new ideas, new alternatives. We can learn so much from others, while remaining our own unique selves.

 Lord, I trust you even more when I see what you do in the lives of your people. Thank you for what they have to teach me. Keep me willing to learn.

What qualities have you appreciated in other people?

■ GET SOME REST

Mark 6:30-31: "Come with me by yourselves to a quiet place and get some rest" (v. 31).

One friend observed about her life: "Everything seems so hectic lately—owning a home, having to drive everywhere, answering the phone that never seems to stop ringing. My life is frantic and chaotic. I'm trying so hard to get everything done that there's no room for God."

There's one quality of life that's almost entirely missing from many lives—the quality of rest. Real rest changes everything else—our relationships with God, with other people, with ourselves. Several friends have said that they're trying hard to find room for that "rest."

● "It takes thought and planning to balance your life. I'm deciding not to do a lot of things I used to think were necessary."

● "I try to make sure I have time to really listen to the people I live with. If I don't, I'm too busy."

● "We're becoming more reclusive. We set aside whole weekends to escape our tasks, our relatives, and our neighbors' kids."

● "I don't have to do everything in my church or family. I'm learning to rely on the Spirit to let me know what I should and should not do each day."

 Lord, teach me to come away and get some rest.

If your life feels too frantic and hectic, what are you going to do about it?

■ ACCEPTING FORGIVENESS

Ps. 103:6-14:   "As far as the east is from the west, so far has he removed our transgressions from us" (v. 12).

Sometimes, even though I know that God has forgiven me, and I hear the words of forgiveness expressed, I find it hard to forgive myself. The most helpful words I ever found about this come from the autobiography of novelist Elizabeth Goudge, *The Joy of the Snow*:

"We have to learn to forgive ourselves. After the cross, I think that what most convinces us of the love of God is the forgiveness of his sons and daughters. I do not think that love and forgiveness can be separated, since real love, by its very nature, must forgive. To know oneself forgiven by God and by those we love is a most humbling and lovely experience and teaches us the necessity of forgiveness . . . Forgiving others would not be difficult, knowing as we do how great is our own need of it, but forgiving oneself is another matter. There is no one harder to forgive than oneself; it can take years. Nevertheless, we know inside ourselves that it must be done, for remorse is a sin that rots away the very vitals of the soul. And we know well the price of a soul to God. If God and his saints in their divine foolishness put such a price upon our soul, we should not let it rot."

 Lord, you have promised that you forgive us totally. Help me to forgive myself, knowing the price paid for my soul.

Write on a piece of paper some things that bother you. Now burn it. That's what God has done with your sin.

■ LIVING THE QUESTIONS

James 1:2-8: "But when he asks, he must believe and not doubt" (v. 6).

James says that if we ask God for guidance, we must expect to be guided in order to receive from the Lord.

But sometimes we do ask, expecting to be guided, and nothing seems to be happening. How long do we keep expecting? It is not always easy to be hopeful, patient, or undemanding toward ourselves or toward God. Yet this is just what we must try to do.

What helps me most is remembering that we see most of what God does only by hindsight. Even though I know that God is with me in the midst of everything, I still sometimes become anxious and impatient. But I know that when I've gone far enough to look back, I'll see how God has guided and protected me all along. What I can't see now, I will see then.

The poet Rainer Maria Rilke wrote: "Be patient toward all that is unsolved in your heart. And try to love the questions themselves. Do not seek the answers that cannot be given you because you would not be able to live them. Live the questions now. Perhaps you will then gradually, without noticing it, live along some distant day into the answer."

 Lord, when I can't see what you are doing in the present, help me remember what you have done in the past.

Copy the Rilke quote and share it with someone you know would appreciate it.

■ LETTING GO

Ps. 121:7-8: "The Lord will keep you from all harm—he will watch over your life; the Lord will watch over your coming and going both now and forevermore."

Olaf Christiansen used to say with a twinkle in his eye that at night he would pray, "Lord, I've been taking care of the world all day. Now you take over."

All of us need to learn how to let go and let God. Sometimes I need to let go of my own dignity and laugh at myself. I may need to let go of a person and set him free to go his own way. Sometimes it's a problem I have to let go, or my control over an organization, or my fear of the future.

Letting go is often a process rather than a one-time event. I let go, only to take up the burden again. Then I have to repeat the process. But the burden becomes smaller each time, until the letting go is final. I like the words of Adrian van Kaam and Susan Muto:

"Will the earth cease to spin on its axis if we take an hour or two to let the breeze blow through our hair? In that moment of playful surrender, we might experience the Lord at play in the world."

 Lord, keep me from the need to control and solve everything. I can let go because I know that you watch over my coming and going and all that concerns me.

What is there that you need to let go of right now?

■ SACRED IDLENESS

Psalm 46: "Be still, and know that I am God"
(v. 10).

Work is not always required of us. There is such a thing as sacred idleness, the cultivation of which is now fearfully neglected." George Macdonald wrote this more than a century ago, but his words are no less true today.

We live in a world that goads us to produce and achieve. "Time is money." "Look for measurable results." Perhaps most men have always been under this pressure, but today more and more women also feel it.

The pressure to produce may make it difficult for us to take time for "sacred idleness" like prayer. Or if we do pray or meditate, we can fall into the trap of striving for spiritual productivity. Sometimes we need just to sit still and listen, doing nothing, expecting nothing.

Free for a time from what we do, or say, or think, we may find the truer reality at the center of our being—all the unseen possibilities, dreams, and hopes. In such idleness we also find rest, knowing that God has loved us not for anything we did, or said, or thought. He just loves us because he wants to. In such stillness we may discover our true reason for existence: to know God.

 Lord, help me relearn the art of sacred idleness.

How could you make some space in your life for sacred idleness?

■ COMPARING

Matt. 25:14-30: "Well done, good and faithful
servant! You have been faithful with a few things; I
will put you in charge of many things. Come and
share your master's happiness!" (v. 21).

Why did the person in the parable hide his one
talent in the ground? Maybe it was because he looked
at the other two people, with their five and ten
talents, and felt, "What's the use? I'll never be as good
as they are, so I may as well give up."

I can understand that. For years I compared myself
with other Christians around me and always came to
the conclusion that I didn't measure up. A speaker at a
retreat said that too often we think of the Christian life
in athletic terms, such as a race. Then we're
wondering how we're doing compared with others,
what our score is, or whether we're beating our own
record. A better way of thinking, she said, was to
think in terms of flowers. They don't struggle or
strain. They just grow as they were meant to grow—
by receiving the sunshine from the air and the water
from the earth. And flowers don't compare themselves
to one another. A tulip never looks down on a petunia.
Each becomes what it is meant to be.

I'm learning that God doesn't compare me with
others, so I don't have to do that either. I can't even
judge my own progress. But I can rest in God's love
and trust that I am becoming what he intends me to
be.

 Lord, thank you for the joy of being my own
unique self.

**Do you often compare yourself unfavorably with
someone you know? Could you talk about this with
her?**

■ TESTING AUTHORITY

1 Thess. 5:12-28:   "Test everything. Hold on to the good" (v. 21).

The news from Jonestown shocked us—hundreds of men, women, and children following a self-styled prophet into death. How can things like this happen? How can people be so blind?

The complexities of modern life leave many feeling so confused and threatened that often they will gladly follow anyone who says, "I have the truth. Follow me and you'll be safe." Easy targets are women who have suffered loss or tragedy, who are exhausted from stress or overwork, or who are just plain tired from everyday decision making. They can be easily led into accepting the authority of a powerful leader or group.

We need to "test" everything—including the authorities that claim our allegiance. Is this authority open to question? Does it give information and leave us to make the choices? Is it willing to let us be what God wants us to be? Does it help us find power for our lives, rather than taking power over our lives?

If the answer to these questions is *no*, we'd better exercise caution. If the answer is *yes*, we can freely choose to follow this authority, as long as it squares with the will of God as we know it from God's Word and Spirit within us.

Lord, give me good judgment to test the spirits.

Choose one authority in your life and apply the test questions.

■ JUST A HOUSEWIFE

I Tim. 5:25: "Good deeds are obvious, and even those that are not cannot be hidden."

Being a housewife isn't easy these days. As my friend Sue said, "It's pretty depressing when this is all I'm doing and I'm not even doing it well."

Today, women who work outside the home often feel a sense of support, while those of us who choose to be "just housewives" are made to feel that we're wasting our lives.

Probably the word *housewife* doesn't help much. It implies being married to a house—which unfortunately does happen to some women, who then devote their energies to decorating and cleaning a house.

But for most of us, being just a housewife means that we have the time and energy to spend on children, volunteer work, gardening, hospitality, or being a good neighbor. There are as many styles of housewifery as there are paid jobs.

 "Dear God, whose name is love, who in love and with love formed all that is, teach me to see the great worth of those small everyday tasks involved in the care of others. Teach me to see them for what they are: reenactments of the greatest truth there is, the truth of your unfailing care for me and for all that is" (Ernest Boyer).

What is involved in your being "just a housewife," if you are one?

■ THE GOD OF ALL COMFORT

2 Cor. 1:3-11: ". . . and the God of all comfort, who comforts us in all our troubles, so that we can comfort those in any trouble with the comfort we ourselves have received from God" (vv. 3-4).

In his work as a missionary, Paul described hardship as "being under great pressure, far beyond our ability to endure, so that we despaired even of life." To any woman experiencing severe problems, these words would be very realistic.

Many troubled women—divorcees, widows, battered wives, those who are emotionally disturbed, alcoholics, and many others—are finding help in support groups. Those facing a particular problem have a unique ability to comfort and help others with the same problem. In such groups, the members tell their stories and listen to the stories of others. They share helpful ideas and encouragement. Because they are being delivered, they can offer hope.

At times we rugged individualists isolate ourselves when we could be drawn to others and to God. We don't have to rely on ourselves. God's resources are as great as our need.

 Lord, if all is not well with me, give me the courage to admit it. I look to you for comfort and healing. Guide me to the people or group through which you can work in my life.

Talk to someone who belongs to a support group. Ask how it has helped her.

■ LIVING IN CHAPTERS

2 Cor. 6:1-13: "I tell you, now is the time of God's favor, now is the day of salvation" (v. 2).

Sometimes I feel guilty about having a beautiful home and a comfortable life when so many do not have the barest necessities. Part of me would be overjoyed to give away most of it and live simply in an African village or a Christian community.

Yet right now, my main task in life is to raise my children, and where we are is a good place to do that. Someday, we *could* be free of house, car, and other possessions and go to our mission board and say "Here we are, where can you use us?" But now is the time for doing what we are doing now.

It helps me to realize that I don't have to live my whole life all at once. I can accept the stage I'm in. Elton Trueblood calls this "living in chapters."

One chapter for many of us is raising children. Another may involve preparing for a new career and another giving up that career to respond to an entirely different call.

Gregory the Great said, "Holy desires grow by delay." If the call is still there, I can respond when the time is right.

 Lord, help me to appreciate this chapter of my life for what it is and to live it fully and joyfully.

Is there some call in your life that you may have to wait to respond to? Or is it time for you to open a new chapter?

■ KEEPING A JOURNAL

Luke 2:15-20: "But Mary treasured up all these things and pondered them in her heart" (v. 19).

Mary is the model of the Christian contemplative—the person who reflects deeply on the meaning of her life in the light of God's truth. Many are finding that one of the most helpful tools for reflection and spiritual growth is the personal journal.

A journal is simply a notebook in which you write freely about the events, ideas, struggles, and dreams of your daily life. Writing helps to focus your thinking—clarifies your values and goals. It can help you understand yourself and others. Used along with prayer and spiritual reading, it can lead you to perceive more clearly God's will for your life.

Many women begin keeping a journal during a crisis, like a serious health problem, or the break-up of a marriage. It can help defuse painful emotions and sort out confused thinking. The benefits are so great that they continue the journal, especially to clarify goals and discover new dreams and visions.

A teacher of journal writing, Metta Winter, summarizes: "The personal journal is a private space of quiet and solitude: a place to befriend yourself and to explore the uniqueness of your life's journey."

 Lord, help me to reflect on the meaning of my life.

Buy a notebook and begin your journal. Read one of the good books on journal keeping and some womens' journals that have been published.

■ TALK THAT BUILDS UP

Eph. 4:29-32: "Do not let any unwholesome talk come out of your mouths, but only what is helpful for building others up according to their needs, that it may benefit those who listen" (v. 29).

She told me their kitchen ceiling was falling down. Why did they ever buy that decrepit house in the first place? Then she had a flat tire on the freeway—a typical excuse. She's always late. And did you see that dress? Imagine someone with her shape wearing *that* color!" Ever catch yourself saying things like that and wondering "Why am I saying this?"

Running down others is a hard habit to break. When I realized how much of it I was doing, I started making a conscious effort to say kind things about my friends instead. I knew I enjoyed being with people who usually focused on the good things about others. They left me feeling full of energy because conversation that builds others up really does "benefit those who listen."

There's an old Arabian proverb: When you are tempted to say something about another, make the story go through three narrow gates: Is it true? Is it necessary? Is it kind? If the story can pass through all these gates, you may tell it without fear.

 Lord, help me remember that what I say makes a difference. Teach me to use words that truly build up others.

Think of someone about whom you have said many unkind things. Declare a moratorium on talking about her for a while, until you can break the habit.

■ CAN PEACE BE ONE-SIDED?

Lev. 19:17:   "Do not bear a grudge against anyone, but settle your differences . . . " (TEV).

In spite of all our desire for reconciliation, there will be times when peacemaking is one-sided. There are words of peace that we will never speak and words of peace that we will never hear, either because the opportunity is past or because human limitations are too great. But healing, if not reconciliation, must take place somehow if we are to go on as whole and healthy people.

Is one-sided peace possible? It is if we realize there are times when peace no longer depends on our actions and that we cannot control the actions of others. We are responsible for doing all the good we can, because hostility may ultimately be overcome with good, but never with hostility. Once we've done all we can, we leave the peacemaking to God. Leaving it to God may mean accepting brokenness because it is part of life. But beyond this, if we are willing to trust God, he can heal our painful memories. God can also, in his own time, change the hearts of people in ways that we cannot imagine or foresee. For our own healing, we must be willing to let go of hate, of hurt, but never of hope.

 Lord, I think of _____. Please heal the memories that hurt and help me leave the relationship in your hands.

Think about a person with whom you do not feel at peace. Are there words that you could yet speak?

■ HE WILL WIPE AWAY EVERY TEAR

Rev. 21:1-4: "He will wipe away every tear from their eyes. There will be no more death or mourning or crying or pain, for the old order of things has passed away" (v. 4).

Some people today are preaching a Christianity of prosperity, easy answers, and total peace of mind. For many who are tired of thinking about how to live and weary of facing a needy and despairing world, this has great appeal. The only problem is that God has not promised us simple answers, unlimited wealth, instant solutions, or freedom from suffering—not in this world.

But look what he has promised us:
- We are his daughters, people of his kingdom.
- We receive the strength to do anything he calls us to do.
- God deeply and eternally loves us.
- We need never go through anything alone, because he is with us always.

These are promises we can trust throughout this life. The longer we live, the more we find that they are better than the glittering but false promises of wealth, success, and easy answers.

And beyond this life we look forward to an even greater time when God's will is fully done, when the old order has passed away. Then, fully in God's presence, we will find that "he will wipe away every tear. . . . There will be no more death or mourning or crying or pain."

 Lord, what can we say in the face of such promises but thanks, thanks, and again thanks.

Make a list of the promises of God that have meant the most to you.

■ SPIRITUAL READING

Col. 3:15-17: "Let the word of Christ dwell in you richly . . . " (v. 16).

The Bible, Christian books from the past and present, plays, poetry, novels—all can serve as spiritual reading, reading we do to open ourselves to God's transforming power.

How can you find the spiritual reading that is right for you? One friend asks people, "Where have you been finding light?" Talk to people of denominations other than your own; they may know of good books that you have not heard of. Look in the bibliographies of books that you have liked. Ask your local Christian bookseller or church librarian. Assemble a library of your own. It doesn't have to be large, just available so you can pull something off the shelf when you need it, or to share with a friend.

Some basic attitudes have helped me in my reading: Take what you can use; you don't need to argue with or criticize the rest. Don't let yourself be intimidated; accept yourself for who and where you are, without comparing yourself with the writer. If a book doesn't speak to you, leave it and try again later; something you aren't ready for now may be very helpful five years from now.

 Lord, speak to me through your Word and the words of those whose lives have been lived close to you.

Gather several favorite and several new books where you can read from them even if you have only a few minutes.

■ A WILLING SPIRIT

Psalm 51: "Restore to me the joy of your salvation and grant me a willing spirit" (v. 12).

What do you do when you have really messed up? When you feel trapped in some sin that is ruining your life? When you are desperate for the power of God? Having committed adultery with Bathsheba and been confronted by the prophet Nathan, David *knew* he needed help.

David's attitude reveals the way for us when we need God's grace. He expressed gratitude and praise for what God had already done for him. He was willing to admit his wrong, without making any excuses. He admitted that it was not only a sin against other people, but against God. He was willing to be changed, asking God to purge him, to give him a clean heart and a right spirit. He exprèssed confidence that God would and could restore him. He promised to share with others whatever God taught him.

When we fall into sin or fall short of what we know to be God's will for us, if we turn to God like David, we too will receive forgiveness, joy, and new life. The only sacrifice that God wants is a repentant heart and a willingness to be changed.

 "Create in me a pure heart, O God, and renew a steadfast spirit within me" (v.10).

Identify some sin in your life. Write out each of the six steps outlined in the psalm as it applies to your situation.

■ PERSONAL PRONOUNS

John 17:6-26: "All I have is yours, and all you have is mine. And glory has come to me through them" (v.10).

Martin Luther said, "The heart of religion lies in the personal pronouns." Religion implies a personal bond, a belonging to God. Jesus referred to *my* Father, *my* sheep, *my* disciples. We say, "*My* God, *my* Savior."

Today the controversy rages over which pronouns to use when referring to God or to other Christians. In the past, all Christians were "sons of God," and we were encouraged to love our "brothers." Most people today have little trouble saying that there are also "daughters" of God.

The real controversy comes over the nouns and pronouns that refer to God. Most of the time, the Bible uses masculine words like king, Lord, Father, and refers to God with masculine pronouns. Some women dislike this language and would rather refer to God as "she" or "Mother." Other women feel just as strongly that they do not want the traditional language changed. Perhaps the majority of women can tolerate both approaches.

God, of course, is neither male nor female, although Jesus was a male. Asking "what gender is God?" is a little like asking "what color is God?" The important thing is that God is personal to each of us, no matter which pronouns most comfortably convey that message to us.

Lord, I thank you that I know you are *my* God, no matter what other pronouns are used.

Ask some friends whose opinions you do not already know how they feel about the use of masculine and feminine language in religion.

■ CONFESSION

James 5:13-16:   "Therefore confess your sins to each other and pray for each other so that you may be healed" (v. 16).

Dietrich Bonhoeffer wrote: "He who is alone with his sin is utterly alone." It is so important that we be able to confess our sin, to admit our wrongdoing and shortcomings. We can always confess to God. But to really accept God's forgiveness, we often need to confess to another human being and receive assurance, face to face, that we are forgiven.

We can confess to our pastor, but how often is this done? Most pastors are male, and many women are uncomfortable discussing some things with a man. Sometimes we need to talk to another woman; with her we experience the presence of God as she hears specific sins and offers personal words of forgiveness and assurance. This is a gift we can give one another. Through confession and prayer for one another, we will find healing.

Unconfessed sin can have destructive power over us; confession diffuses the power of the secret. We leave the old sin behind, having learned what we can from it, and make a new beginning. Bonhoeffer wrote further: "In confession the breakthrough to new life occurs. Where sin is hated, admitted, and forgiven, there the break with the past is made. 'Old things are passed away.' "

 Lord, I thank you for your gift of forgiveness and for those human friends who help me receive it.

Think of another woman, a believer you trust, that you might ask to listen to your confession.

74

■ GROWTH THROUGH SUFFERING

Isaiah 53:   "Surely he took up our infirmities and carried our sorrows" (v. 4).

To herself and others, Debbie had always seemed confident and capable. Now in the middle of a divorce, she says the hardest thing is that everyone expects her to "handle it well" when in fact she feels she is falling apart.

Many think that in a crisis Christians should not feel bad or should manage well because of their faith, but this is not always true. What is true for the Christian is that in the midst of crisis, God enters in a significant and obvious way.

Crisis often makes us numb—we feel isolated from ourselves, others, and God. We may not *sense* the nearness or power of God at all. Until it is an honest statement, we don't have to say anything positive about our suffering, like "This must be part of God's plan for me" or "I know I'll be a better person when this is over." We are free to feel as bad, manage as poorly, be as confused, out of control, incompetent, and needy as we are.

Our greatest resource is not ourselves, but God's grace. In the midst of our greatest failure and weakness God says, "You are not defeated. You are not alone. I am still with you."

 Dear Lord, your coming into our lives often follows suffering, but you always come with strength.

In a crisis, allow yourself to experience your own weakness and failure, and trust in God's sustaining presence.

■ BECOMING

Luke 19:1-10: "For the Son of Man came to seek and to save what was lost" (v. 10).

Many voices today encourage us to become "who we are." For Christian women, this happens as we come into the presence of Jesus.

Zacchaeus climbed into a tree and ended up inviting Jesus to his house for supper. In that meeting, Zacchaeus saw himself as he really was because, in the presence of Jesus, he saw what he could be. Through Jesus' loving acceptance, he started on the road to becoming his best self.

Louis Evely wrote: "We only grow well for those by whom we are loved. We are grateful to a person who loves us because he has believed sufficiently in us to enable us to dare be with him so much better, so much more affectionate, so much more vulnerable, more generous than we would have been with anyone else."

Jesus believes in us. He knows each of us, searches for us, and calls us by name. His love awakens our love. Like Zacchaeus, by being with Jesus we are changed, and we begin to become "who we are."

 Lord, thank you for your love, which calls forth the best that is in me.

In what ways do you come into the presence of Jesus?

■ THE DESIRES OF YOUR HEART

Ps. 37:4: "Seek your happiness in the Lord, and he will give you your heart's desire" (TEV).

Some people have the idea that if they really enjoy doing something, God probably wants them to be doing something else. They see God's will as hard, painful, against our natural inclinations. But as a loving Father, God has chosen to give us certain gifts, and what we are good at is often an important clue to our calling in life. It is one of the clearest ways we can know God's will.

For that reason, it's good to identify these natural gifts, the "desires of your heart." They will be truly yours, not what someone else wants. They will not be a wrong desire that could harm someone else. It's not wrong to desire a certain career, or one volunteer job instead of another. If the goal is in agreement with the will of God as you know it, you can "commit your way to the Lord" and move ahead. Trust God's promise that he will give you what you desire.

Glenn Clark wrote: "Gifts of God always bring peace, contentment, and joy, and therefore anything in which I find a natural harmony and peace and which does not interfere with anyone else's expression of life belongs to me, and any work for which I feel a natural call, by gift or inclination, is mine to do."

 Lord, you call us ahead by placing desires in our hearts. Help us to recognize what we truly desire.

How would you complete the sentence "If I could be anything I wanted to, I'd be . . ."?

■ GOOD ADVISORS

Prov. 15:21-24: "Plans fail for lack of counsel, but with many advisers they succeed" (v. 22).

God guides us through the counsel of others. For example, in making a career choice, you will want to think about your own abilities and goals. But then you could talk to other women about their experiences. Career aptitude programs can help identify possibilities that you may not have considered. Family and friends may have ideas, and it's worth listening to them just because they know you so well. A pastor or professional counselor may help you sort out some of the tensions between family and work. Your best friends will pray for you.

As the proverb suggests, many advisers are an aid to success. They can prevent us from being unduly influenced by our own wishful thinking or by one strong friend or family member. Even with many advisers, you have to make your own decision, but you can do that depending on God's promise "I will instruct you and teach you in the way you should go; I will counsel you and watch over you" (Ps. 32:8).

 Lord, help me find the advisers I need.
Through them, guide me with your counsel.

If you have a decision to make or a problem to solve, make a list of those who might be able to give you good advice.

■ BELIEVE AND RECEIVE

Mark 11:12-24: "Whatever you ask for in prayer, believe that you have received it, and it will be yours" (v. 24).

You and your friend have had a nasty argument. You try to imagine what will happen next time you meet. You play and replay in your mind all the upsetting things that will be said. Another disastrous encounter seems inevitable.

It isn't. You can make a conscious decision that things will be different, but you must bring your deep, emotional levels—your subconscious—into agreement or it will work against you.

There is a way of praying that some call "affirmations." It involves quietly repeating positive, faith-filled phrases over and over until they take root in the deepest levels of our being. We are acting in *faith*, choosing to dwell not on our fears, but on the positive results we desire.

For example, each time you think of your friend, you could say one of these statements several times:

"I release my fear of her anger and affirm that God is bringing healing between us."

"I send blessings and love to her."

"Thank you, Lord, that you are pouring your transforming love into both my friend and me."

 Lord, teach me to fill my mind and heart with your promises.

Think of one difficult situation you are facing. Create affirmations that remind you that God is answering your prayers.

■ THE BATTLE AGAINST EVIL

Psalm 3: "O Lord, how many are my foes! How many rise up against me! Many are saying of me, 'God will not deliver him' " (vv. 1-2).

One of the reasons the psalms are a favorite part of the Bible is that they are so realistic. They never pretend that all is well. They recognize that life is a battle against evil—evil in the world and in ourselves.

In the battle, other people hurt us. Our children may do terrible things even if we have been good mothers. The nightmares of alcoholism, drug addiction, and sudden illness attack our friends and our own families. We may feel as if the whole world is falling apart. Yet, like David, we trust in God and cry to him for help. We trust that beyond the absence, there is a presence. Beyond the pain, there is healing. Beyond the brokenness, there is wholeness. Beyond the anger, there will be peace. Beyond the hurting, there is forgiveness. Beyond the silence, there is the Word. Through the Word, there may be understanding. Through understanding, there is love.

The resurrection is the ultimate evidence of God's resourcefulness and power, of his ability to bring life out of death. Because of Easter, we know that "darkness and sin and evil can never again have the last word" (Leslie Weatherhead).

 God, so often you have transformed hurt into blessing. But it's hard to trust. Help me.

Can you remember a time in your life when good came out of suffering?

■ AUTHORITY AND SUBMISSION

Eph. 5:21-33: "Submit to one another out of
reverence for Christ" (v. 21).

A psychologist in California reported that her office is
full of women whose lives are a shambles over the
issue of authority and submission in marriage. At one
end of the scale are women whose husbands are
expecting them to play a submissive role they cannot
accept. At the opposite end are women who are
pressuring their husbands to be more authoritarian.
Either way the question is the same: "Who's the
boss?"

Jesus' approach is to say, "That's the wrong
question." The issue is not "Who has authority?" but
"Who is the servant?" Jesus raises the question to a
different level—the level of service. "Whoever wants
to become great among you must be your servant, and
whoever wants to be first must be slave of all" (Mark
10:43-44). Neither husband nor wife is to dominate the
other, but to have the other's best interests at heart.

Letha Scanzoni and Nancy Hardesty summarize:
"All of us as Christians are called to forsake the ways
of the world, which includes dominion and lording it
over others (Mark 10:42). We are to be subject to one
another out of reverence for Christ (Eph. 5:21). . . In
Christ there is no chain of command, but a community
founded and formed by self-giving love."

 Lord, help me to serve others—male and
female—the way you have served us.

What would it mean to "submit" to one another in a
healthy marriage or other relationship?

FROM CRITICISM TO ENCOURAGEMENT

Matt. 7:1-5: "Do not judge, or you too will be judged" (v. 1).

Years ago, when my friend Susan had left her husband and filed for a divorce, my first reaction was critical. Why is she taking the easy way out? Why can't she try harder to make it work? Is she just getting a divorce because it's the current fad?

When I had a chance to sit down and talk with her and hear her side of the story, I realized how unfair I had been. I knew that if I had experienced what she had, I might have done the same thing. How easily I had judged, and on the basis of too little information. So often we don't really know the pain and stress that other people are going through. And our condemnation and lack of understanding only adds to their pain.

After that experience, I decided that I would try to be a better friend, a fellow sufferer rather than a judge. I know that I can go to God with my sins and weaknesses and find forgiveness and acceptance. I want to offer that same gift to others. Without people to whom we can speak safely and honestly, we cannot work through our difficulties.

William Penn said, "Inquire often, but judge rarely, and thou wilt not often be mistaken."

 Lord, forgive my tendency to judge others. Help me to forgive and accept, the way you forgive and accept me.

Do you find it easy or difficult to listen to other people without telling them what you think they should do?

■ THE OPPRESSED

Psalm 10:   "You hear, O Lord, the desire of the afflicted; you encourage them, and you listen to their cry, defending the fatherless and the oppressed, in order that man, who is of the earth, may terrify no more" (vv. 17-18).

Oppression happens whenever people are put down, treated as nonpersons, when their feelings or needs are ignored. This can happen to women, to children, to old people, and, yes, to men.

When Jesus came, he announced that one of his tasks was to "release the oppressed" (Luke 4:18). We can share in that work—beginning in our own homes, by valuing our own children and treating them and their ideas with respect. We can pay attention to those whom society ignores—the fatherless, the poor (who are often women), the old (who are also more often women). We can work through an organization like Amnesty International to counteract oppression in the world. In doing so, we become coworkers with God: "He will defend the afflicted among the people and save the children of the needy; he will crush the oppressor" (Ps. 72:4).

 Show me, O Lord, what I can do for the oppressed.

The imprecatory psalms take on new meaning for us when we pray them on behalf of the oppressed. This week pray psalms such as 139, 137, or 69 from this perspective.

■ HONEST SHARING

Eph. 4:25-28: "Therefore each of you must put off falsehood and speak truthfully to his neighbor, for we are all members of one body" (v. 25).

Some people are always "fine." We never hear much about their problems, or we get the impression that God solves them all instantly.

Others are "crabby Christians." They'll complain about their problems and hardships as long as we'll listen. Their difficulties seem insoluble, even for God.

We Christians need one another—but not to give one another either easy answers or headaches. We need to share both our strength and our struggle.

Our strength gives strength to others—what's going well for us, what we're grateful for, the helpful books we've discovered, the truths that have suddenly become "truer" for us, the specific ways that God is working in our lives.

But we also share our failures, doubts, and questions. In struggling together, we also help one another. And that is always our aim, the reason for speaking truthfully to our neighbor, as members of the same body.

Lord, send me people who will tell me the truth about their Christian lives. Bring me together with those who have something to say that I need to hear.

Which do you tend to talk about most—your problems or your blessings?

■ GOD'S WORKS ARE PERFECT

Phil.1:3-11: "Being confident of this, that he who began a good work in you will carry it on to completion until the day of Christ Jesus" (v. 6).

Every day I see people jogging past my living room windows—trying to overcome stress, fatigue, and excess weight. There must be days when they're tempted to give up, but they believe that eventually they'll experience the benefits. Sometimes it seems as if my efforts at spiritual "fitness" are taking up a lot of time and not much is happening. "Progress is too slow," I say to myself. "Over and over I make the same mistakes. I'm tired of reading the same ideas, praying the same prayers, wanting to change and having the same old defects."

What do I hold on to when I feel this way?

I remind myself that growth is often too slow to see except by hindsight; sometimes I never see it, but others do. I also know that temptation, suffering, and limitation will always be with me; I won't be "complete" until the day of Christ Jesus. But even though I'll never "arrive," it's good just to be on the road. Best of all, I can trust God to finish what he has started. Because God doesn't give up on me, neither do I.

 Lord, our works aren't perfect until they're complete. But yours are perfect all along. Remind me that I'm *your* work.

Make a list of all the things you're doing right.

■ WOMEN IN THE CHURCH

Phil. 4:1-3: ". . . these women . . . have contended at my side in the cause of the gospel, along with Clement and the rest of my fellow workers, whose names are in the book of life" (v. 3).

Paul is often blamed for relegating women to second-class citizenship in the church—but that's not the whole story. In his letter to the Christians at Philippi he mentions two women, Euodia and Synteche, speaking of them as co-workers who "contended at my side in the cause of the gospel."

The culture in the first century was much different from ours; the early church in some ways reflected that culture and accommodated itself to it. The same is true today. In many denominations, women are taking a more active role, both as pastors and lay persons. While barriers remain, more and more women are able to find ways in which their gifts can be used in the church. With that freedom goes the responsibility of making wise choices. We need to ask questions like, "Is this a worthwhile project or activity?" "Do I have the abilities needed for the task?" "How can I best serve in this church?"

 Lord, I thank you for the privilege of sharing the gospel. Help me find the best use of my unique gifts.

How do you see your role as a woman in the church? Is it any different from that of the men in your church?

■ SELF-FULFILLMENT OR SELF-DENIAL

Luke 9:23-24: "Whoever loses his life for me will save it" (v. 24).

What did Jesus mean when he said that you have to lose your life in order to save it? Does this mean I have to give up my hopes for happiness, my sense of self-esteem, my desire for self-fulfillment? In meeting the needs of others, do I have to completely forget my own needs?

Paul Tournier wrote: "Many people have quite a negative conception of Christianity, as if it consisted in continual self-amputation, as if God wanted to hold us down, rather than that we should 'turn again and live.'"

"To lose your life" doesn't mean to lose your true identity or deny your gifts. It means to lose your old self, your false selves, in order to become the person God means you to be. God does not want us to be miserable failures or self-pitying martyrs. He wants us to grow and develop so that we have more to give in service to others. We grow as we remain in close contact with Jesus. We have his promise: "I am the vine, and you are the branches. Whoever remains in me, and I in him, will bear much fruit" (John 15:5 TEV).

 Lord, shall we not bring these gifts to your service? Shall we not bring to your service all our powers. . .?" (T. S. Eliot).

What aspects of your self do you need to "lose" in order to find true life?

87

■ TEMPTATION OR OPPORTUNITY

1 Cor. 10:13:   "And God is faithful; he will not let you be tempted beyond what you can bear. But when you are tempted, he will also provide a way out so that you can stand up under it."

Each of us faces her own array of temptations. For some it might be the temptation to gossip. For another the need to control or find fault. Or the temptation to ignore the needs of others, to greed, to unfaithfulness. Our temptations are as unique as our fingerprints.

Temptation is really a time for choosing. Our values aren't really ours until we have to make some choices based on them. Every day we either give in to temptation or choose according to our values. The one leads to brokenness, the other to wholeness.

Theologian Eugene Kennedy says that wholeness comes not just from resisting temptation, but from choosing the course that demands more of oneself. "We are fulfilled not, as some contemporaries suggest, by giving in to temptation in the name of fuller human experience; nor are we fulfilled . . . by backing away from life and its dangers. We are fulfilled as we find ourselves through making positive choices that demand more of ourselves. Temptation is an opportunity to make a commitment to one's better self, to one's possibilities for the fulness of life that is promised to all Christians."

 O Lord, let sin never ensnare us with its empty promises. Make us one with you always, so that we may be whole.

The most powerful weapon in the face of temptation is God's Word. Read Matt. 4:1-11; Eph. 6:10-18; and Heb. 4:14-16.

■ SAYING NO

Eph. 2:1-10: "For we are God's workmanship, created in Christ Jesus to do good works, which God prepared in advance for us to do" (v. 10).

An unemployed friend has now turned down two jobs that would have been financially rewarding because neither of them is what she feels called to do. Her husband is beginning a new business, and they have little money, but she still says no.

For her there's a difference between work you *can* do and work you *must* do. Just because you're good at something or because you can make money doing it doesn't mean it's your true work.

For years men have been in the trap of measuring their worth in terms of money or prestige. Now many women are jumping headlong into the same trap: "I have worth because I can accomplish something or make a certain amount of money." A job or income can add to our sense of worth, but it is not the basis.

Our worth comes not from what we *do* but from what we *are*. The law says, "You're good if you perform well." God's grace says, "You're good because God has redeemed you." Grace sets us free from the need to make choices based on law, free to say no—or yes.

 Lord, I'm thankful that my worth doesn't depend on my performance, but it is founded on your grace.

If you could choose any work to do, regardless of money or prestige, what would it be? Is there any way you could include this work in your life, if you haven't already?

■ EVERYDAY TASKS

Prov. 31:10-29: "She watches over the affairs of her household and does not eat the bread of idleness" (v. 27).

Although my list of everyday tasks is not the same, I feel a kinship with this ancient woman. Much of my life, too, is spent doing common tasks.

A friend said, "I find it easy to believe in God's care when something good happens. And strangely enough, I feel close to God when my back is to the wall and I say 'God, help me!' because he always comes through. But my real problem is with the dull gray areas of daily life. That's when I forget God."

One dull gray day I found this prayer stuck in a book:

"O God, you who are love, release me from the chill in my own heart. Days and weeks pass, and I remain locked into my own self, and find no way out to others. Let the simple deeds I perform in my everyday work reach and support someone, even if it be only one person. You have woven us all together, and you see the threads that bind into an invisible fellowship the tired and the strong, the fainthearted and the brave. I know that I am in your hand, and I know that I daily receive good gifts from many who find it harder to believe than I do. Take my ordinary everyday actions and send them where you will."

Copy out this prayer, and place it where you can read it when you feel the "dailiness."

■ SAVED FROM SIN

Matt. 1:18-23:   "She will give birth to a son, and you are to give him the name Jesus, because he will save his people from their sins" (v. 21).

When we hear the word *sin*, we still have a tendency to think of wrongdoing, of bad acts. Yet these are only the surface symptoms of sin; the roots lie much deeper. Georgia Harkness described sin as our "biological tendency to self-centeredness." A degree of self-centeredness is needed for self-preservation and for growth, but as it passes into selfishness and self-love, it becomes the root of sin and unhappiness.

What are some signs that legitimate self-interest has crossed the boundary into sin? Harkness suggests these: the desire to have our own way regardless of the wishes and needs of others; the narrowing of interests to what immediately touches us; a thirst for personal recognition, compliments, and applause; an eagerness in conversation or action always to occupy the center of the stage; jealousy of others who secure recognition or privileges or anything good that we want; self-pity, peevishness, or complaining when things do not go as we would like to have them.

The desire for achievement and self-development is good, but not when it becomes a selfish focus on ourselves. Jesus came to save us from that sin. In a paradoxical way, he frees us from the bondage to self so that we can become our very best selves.

 Lord, let me leave my values and viewpoints behind if they are not yours.

Which of the signs of sinful self-love do you recognize in yourself?

■ OUR FATHER

Matt. 6:5-15:   "This is how you should pray: 'Our Father in heaven. . . .' " (v. 9).

Dorothy shook her head. "I just can't pray to God as Father. For me, *father* means the person who abused us and then abandoned the family." Dorothy is one of many women saying they have difficulty thinking of God as Father because they did not have loving human fathers. And for those who had fathers who set unreasonable standards, or who were undemonstrative, or just too busy, that picture may not be most helpful. The Bible has many others.

But perhaps we should not be too quick to abandon the image of God as Father. Having a loving father is a basic need of all children, and maybe women who did not have one in childhood especially need to know that they are loved by a true Father. This Father will never abandon us. He is never too busy to listen. He loves us and wants us to be happy and knows what will make us happy.

Even women who had less-than-ideal human fathers can dare to pray "Our Father." When we pray *Our* Father, we are joined with all other women—and men—as children of this all-loving God.

 Lord, we thank you that we can call you our Father.

Use a concordance to find the biblical references to God as Father.

■ TODAY IS THE DAY

Matt. 6:25-34: "Therefore do not worry about tomorrow, for tomorrow will worry about itself. Each day has enough trouble of its own'" (v. 34).

A woman at a retreat told how for years she had bottled up her resentment and anger at her ex-husband. Just as she was learning to express those feelings, she became a Christian and realized she needed to forgive her husband. "But I don't want to forgive him," she exclaimed. "I just got angry!"

This woman knew that she had to let go of her anger about the past to live freely and positively in the present. Some of us have more trouble with fear of the future. Planning ahead is fine, but not if we begin to anticipate the emotions of the future today. God gives us strength only for what is happening right now.

We labor and are heavy laden when we carry the burdens of the past or of the future. The only burden we can do anything about is that of this day. Trying to solve the problems of the past or the future with today's energy leads only to exhaustion. We focus our energy on what we, with God's help, are going to do about today. Then, when we have done that, we are to lay aside anxiety, and rest.

 Lord, grant me the serenity to accept *today* the things I cannot change, the courage to change *today* the things I can, and the wisdom *today* to know the difference.

Are you carrying any burdens of the past or future that you can let go of *today*?

■ LONELINESS AND ALIENATION

Matt. 28:16-20: "And surely I will be with you
always, to the very end of the age" (v. 20).

All women at times experience loneliness—the ache
of losing a close friend or a husband, separation from
friends or family when we move, the feeling of
isolation and disconnectedness from other people
during a crisis. A woman can experience loneliness in
the midst of her family if she begins to feel like a cog
in the machinery. She keeps everyone else's plans and
activities going, but wonders, "Who am I?" We can
feel lonely even in a crowd, like a wedding or class
reunion, when we can't connect with anyone there.

Loneliness is uncomfortable, but loneliness and
aloneness are not the same. No matter what our
situation, there is always a part of us that is unique,
independent, and alone. No one—except God—can
ever know us completely. To some extent we are
always "a stranger and alone." Instead of succumbing
to self-pity over this, we can learn to accept this lone
center in our lives and value it.

Ronald V. Wells wrote: "Such acceptance leads to a
dawning awareness of what it means to be in
possession of this enduring center—ourselves in our
aloneness. There is no fear here. There can be the
beginning discovery of power and strength which
sustains us in solitude. Then it becomes abundantly
clear: here is the place where God meets us."

 Lord, in my aloneness, may I experience your
presence.

**When do you feel lonely? When do you feel alone—
just being yourself, just being with God?**

■ WOUNDED HEALERS

2 Cor. 1:3-7: "God . . . comforts us in all our troubles, so that we can comfort those in any trouble with the comfort we ourselves have received from God" (v. 4).

As Sheri was talking with a friend about forgiving, she realized that there was someone she needed to forgive too. She did it, and it changed her life.

Another woman lost a friend. In the months following, she became close to several other women who had experienced something similar. They helped each other learn to live with their losses.

A woman who had a radical mastectomy now visits other women who are about to have this surgery. She is able to reassure them, and in the process finds new meaning for her life and new friendships.

Often we help others, not out of our strengths, but out of our weakness, by sharing our own struggle and the strength, comfort, and hope that we have received from God.

If we focus on ourselves and our problems, we can grow depressed. But when we are willing to take part in the healing of others, our wounds are healed. Others are transformed and so are we.

 Lord, reveal to us how we might serve as a guide for other fearful and struggling people.

List some of your struggles. How has God helped you in your weakness? How could you extend this help to others?

■ TRUE ASSERTIVENESS

2 Tim. 1:3-7: "God did not give us a spirit of
timidity, but a spirit of power, of love and of self-
discipline" (v. 7).

Some traditional stereotypes see women as passive,
dependent, noncompetitive, submissive, vain, easily
influenced, and in need of security. Is that the way
God intends *any* Christian to be? Paul said that God
has not given us a spirit of timidity—but a spirit of
power, love, and self-discipline. These are the traits
that should develop from our faith—the faith that
Timothy had learned from his grandmother Lois and
his mother Eunice.

The alternative to timidity is power, but Christian
power is not a harsh demand for rights, uncontrolled
ambition, or the use of others. Christian power is
characterized by *love* and *self-discipline*. This is the
kind of power we see in Jesus—not military power,
not aggressiveness, but the strength of self-controlled
love. It is the meek, God promised, who will inherit
the earth (Matt. 5:5).

In *The Lord*, Romano Guardini describes the meek:
"those who have become quiet within, humble and
kind. Theirs is an attitude of genuine selflessness,
clarity, and quiet before God. In the order of things to
come, they will be masters, ruling not with weakness,
but with that strength become mild, which is capable
of ruling straight from the center of truth."

 Lord, through the work of your Spirit within me,
give me a power that is characterized by love
and self-discipline.

**Think of one situation in which you are tempted to be
timid or passive. Ask God to show you how to
respond with loving, self-disciplined power.**

■ INTENTIONAL LIVING

Ps. 130:5-6: "I wait for the Lord, my soul waits, and in his word I put my hope" (v. 5).

Sometimes I find myself thinking, "I can't know what God wants me to do, and even if I did it would probably be too hard or I might not want to do it. If I muddle along, some of what I'm doing will probably be God's will anyway. And none of it is exactly *wrong*."

Disobedience doesn't have to be doing what's wrong. It can also be forgetting to take a rest from doing everything our own way. To wait on God means to cease activity.

Three women wrote a wonderful cookbook called *Laurel's Kitchen*. They describe what happened to them as they began to wait and meditate each morning: "We began to take careful stock of everything to see if we were doing what we really wanted to—the kind of work we did, the parties we went to, the causes we supported, the books we read. One involvement after another fell away, replaced by something better, or not replaced at all except by a little more time, a little more peace of mind."

 Lord, it often seems like wasting time to rest and seek your direction. Teach me what a difference it can make in my life.

Are you spending time on things that you really do not want to be doing? List some things you *want* to do, even if they seem impossible right now.

■ TRUE EQUALITY

Gal. 3:26-29: "There is neither Jew nor Greek, slave nor free, male nor female, for you are all one in Christ Jesus" (v. 28).

A pioneer woman, Joanna L. Stratton, wrote: "In the 19th century, the home was regarded as the proper 'place' for women in society, a sphere where women were expected to serve diligently as wives, mothers and housekeepers. . . . To the pioneer woman, home and hearth meant work loads that were heavier than ever. And yet that work was the work of survival . . . . Men and women worked together as partners, combining their strengths and talents to provide food and clothing for themselves and their children. As a result, women found themselves on a far more equal footing with their spouses."

Our contemporary society needs its men and women working together as partners, combining their strengths and talents, rather than limiting themselves to stereotyped roles. There are still many obstacles to be overcome before men and women are freed to use their God-given gifts. Practical steps will have to be taken by employers, and changes in family life-style worked out. But we have made progress, and can make progress, knowing that in Christ Jesus, God has overcome the barriers between male and female.

 Lord, help me maintain a spirit of cooperation, harmony, and true equality in all my dealings with men.

What changes in our society do you think need to be made so that men and women are free to contribute equally?

■ WHERE IS IT GOING?

John 3:8:   "The wind blows wherever it pleases.
You hear its sound, but you cannot tell where it
comes from or where it is going."

In *The Second Stage* Betty Friedan describes the
corrections she thinks are needed if the potential of
the women's movement is to be realized and women
are not to turn back for fear of the uncertainties and
instabilities of the future.

In many ways, the women's movement has left us
with more questions than answers. We may wonder
where it's really going. But we do feel a sense of
satisfaction about the progress that has been made.
We rejoice in the new possibilities springing up.

Spiritual life is like that. It's not a state we achieve,
but a movement toward God. It's a journey, but we
never in this life arrive. We're always correcting our
course. Paul Tournier says, "That is why Jesus Christ
compared the spirit to the wind, of which one does
not know 'whence it cometh and whither it goeth,' to a
force that passes, which cannot be laid hold of by the
hands, and yet which quenches our thirst for the
Absolute."

All of our lives have been changed by what has been
happening for women in the last 20 years. As in the
life of faith, much of it "cannot be laid hold of." There
is much disagreement and a lot of work left to do. But
that is not a sign of failure, but of life, health, and
hope.

 Lord, keep us from fear of the uncertainties of
life. Instead, help us see possibility and
opportunity.

**What choices have you made that your mother and
grandmother did not have?**

■ WASTING TIME

Eph. 5:15-17: "Make good use of every opportunity you have, because these are evil days" (v. 16 TEV).

Some women are deciding that they are no longer going to waste time in relationships that don't go anywhere, on organizations that serve only to maintain themselves, on bridge parties and gossip. Especially in midlife, both women and men can sense that time is running out.

It's a paradox, but sometimes the best use of time is to waste time—that is, to use it in ways that do not seem immediately productive. Someone has said, "We waste time with those we love." Sometimes I need to waste time with my children, just sitting still and listening to their chattering when *they* need to talk. Sometimes I need to waste time on myself, learning to play again or just sitting in the backyard and enjoying the sunshine. I even need to waste time with God— just being in his presence, without praying, or thinking, or reading.

Such time wasting restores my perspective and renews my energy so I can go back to "making the best use of my time."

 Lord, help me to know when wasting time is the best use of my time.

Today, deliberately choose to waste some time on yourself or someone you love.

■ AN UNCONDITIONAL YES

Mark 1:16-20: "Without delay he called them, and they left their father Zebedee in the boat with the hired men and followed him" (v. 20).

Do your prayers sometimes sound like this: "Lord, help me get along with my husband and still get my own way most of the time." "Lord, help me lose weight and still have food at the center of my life." "Lord, when my daughter-in-law becomes the kind of wife I think my son should have, I'll try to be nice to her."

Because God wants to heal us totally, he does not respond to these attempts at compromise, these halfway measures where we do not admit the sickness of our inner selves. God can heal us only when we are ready to be healed completely—whatever that may mean. Like Simon and Andrew, we must be ready to leave the old ways, our own ways, behind and run the risk of following Jesus totally.

Susan Muto writes: "Spiritual living calls for childlike faith in Christ; I fear the risk. Loving God demands uncompromising surrender; I fear the consequences. I must give all to God, yet how I fear an unconditional yes to God's will. . . I may have to give up my old ways. I wanted to tell God what to do. Now I have to stop telling, and try to listen."

 Lord, by the power of your Spirit, make it possible for me to see where I am sick that I might be made well.

Is there a situation that you've been telling God how to patch up? Are you willing to be healed instead?

■ RELIGION IN ACTION

Isa. 58:6-9: "Is not this the kind of fasting I have chosen: to loose the chains of injustice. . . to share your food with the hungry and to provide the poor wanderer with shelter" (vv. 6-7).

In our country and in the world we are surrounded by real physical poverty, hunger, illiteracy, abuse, and violence. Other more subtle forms of poverty are there too: loneliness, depression, fear. What is our response?

According to Isaiah, our response must go beyond religious rituals—fasting, prayer, or worship. The true "fast" that pleases God is direct service to the poor and the victims of injustice and oppression. This thought is echoed in the New Testament by James: "Religion that God our Father accepts as pure and faultless is this: to look after orphans and widows in their distress. . ." (James 1:27).

The form our "fasting" takes depends on many variables. But we give—out of our overflowing shopping carts, closets, bank accounts, out of our time, empathy, and expertise.

And God is so good to us that we ourselves are blessed in the process: "You will be made rich in every way so that you can be generous on every occasion . . ." (2 Cor. 9:11).

 Lord, make clear to me which needs around me *are* my responsibility, and which are not.

Read *The Caring Question* by Donald Tubesing and Nancy Loving Tubesing.

■ BOTH / AND

Phil. 2:12-13: "Continue to work out your salvation with fear and trembling, for it is God who works in you to will and to act according to his good purpose."

Some people promote the self-help approach to the Christian life: decide what you want to be and go for it. That sounds good until we find out we can't do it.

Others say "You have to realize that you're helpless. Just surrender, and God will do it all." We try that, only to find that God doesn't seem to be doing anything.

What's the answer? We're left with a paradox, like Paul's: "Work out your own salvation, for it is God who works in you."

Peter Gillquist writes: "[God] does not want you sitting idly by, wondering when he will next do something through you. Nor does he want you out hustling up his business, striving to do his will. Instead, learn to live out your union with him, living under his reign in the church, thereby knowing his will and doing what he says to do."

So it's not a question of either/or, but both/and. We trust God and do what we can. "It takes nothing away from God to see him as ultimately trustworthy and yourself as equipped to manage quite well" (Marie Morgan).

 Lord, teach me the balance between trust and initiative.

Are you more tempted to charge ahead under your own power or to be passive and expect God to do it all? Think of one area in which you need a better balance.

■ THE WORK OF OUR HANDS

Psalm 90: "Establish the work of our hands for us—yes, establish the work of our hands" (v. 17).

Speaking to men in 1949, Elton Trueblood wrote: "The man who stays in the secure path, never making the break in the direction of his real interest or sense of calling, will become an increasingly unhappy and frustrated man. The way of wisdom is to make the break and to make it at once in spite of the difficulties and temporary or permanent sacrifice."

Today, more than 30 years later, many women are in exactly the same place, expressing this same need to have a choice about what they will do with their only life. Studies show that mothers who disregard their own needs to "do the right thing" for their families are not as good mothers as those who *want* to be home. Other studies show that whether or not a woman is married, seeking challenging and satisfying work is the best guarantee of happiness and well-being. This work may be motherhood, a career, volunteer work, or any combination thereof. The choice is ours. Women who let others choose for them or who just let life happen to them often end up feeling powerless and depressed. God has given us the freedom to choose our work in the light of the gifts he has given us. We can make that choice, asking God to "establish the work of our hands."

 Help me, Lord, to make wise decisions about the work I will do with my life.

Have you asked your family to sacrifice too little, enough, or too much so that you can do what you feel called to do?

106

■ EFFECTIVE WITNESSES

1 Peter 3:13-17:   "Always be prepared to give an answer to everyone who asks you to give the reason for the hope that you have" (v. 15).

A friend said recently, "It's so hard to find anyone who makes difficult decisions based on faith." I thought, "So many of us do, why don't we say so?"

Some women find it natural to witness. They feel a strong desire to talk about their faith and do it easily. Other women find it hard to put their faith into words. "Give an answer to everyone who asks." How can we do that most effectively?

First of all, Peter says that what we are to do is give a reason for the hope *we* have, share what is real from *our* experience. It's God's job to change the other person.

Secondly, we are to speak with gentleness and respect, never insulting anyone's intelligence and always being sensitive to the feelings of the other person.

Finally Peter mentions the importance of good behavior. Do we ourselves mirror our testimony? Basil Pennington says, "We teach more by what we do and how we live than by what we say, if we want anyone to take us seriously."

 Lord, let some part of my life say something to someone about you.

When was the last time you "gave an answer" to someone?

■ ABUNDANCE

Matt. 25:34-40:   "I tell you the truth, whatever you did for one of the least . . . you did for me" (v. 40).

How often we see a picture of an African mother and her starving child and realize once again how rich we are. Some see our abundance as God's blessing on America, or on themselves. Others feel such pain at the disparity that they can hardly enjoy their blessings.

I'm grateful that I'm American. A life is possible for me that is impossible for many. I thank God for freedom, medical care, good food, my home, and all the rest.

But I know that God doesn't love me any more than the African mother, or the woman in China who is forced by law to work. But she lives there and I live here and that makes a big difference. What am I going to do about it?

It's easy to get caught up in despair and guilt. Instead, I must begin to find the ways that people *are* trying to change things, meanwhile sharing what they can. The Lord who cared about the poor in his lifetime is still doing so through us. The Spirit has moved people to immense creativity and effectiveness in helping others. If I'm willing, I can find out what I can do.

 Lord, I get so caught up in managing my abundance. Help me slow down and be willing to hear what you have to say about sharing it.

In your church and community, you'll find others who have found ways to help. Ask them what you can do.

■ LIGHT IN THE DARKNESS

John 1:1-9: "The light shines in the darkness, and the darkness has never put it out" (v. 5 TEV).

Many women are trying to discover which images of God are most meaningful to them. My favorite is the image of God as *light*. "God is light; in him there is no darkness at all" (1 John 1:5). "I have come into the world as a light, so that no one who believes in me should stay in darkness" (John 12:46).

Light is such a hopeful image. It reminds me of all the places in my life into which God's light has shined—the questions answered, problems resolved, decisions made. I know that what is now in darkness will someday become clear.

The image of light reminds me of people whose lives are bright. "I am the light of the world," said Jesus. And as we reflect his light, we too become the light of the world. We may think that our light is feeble and dim, yet others will be drawn to it and find warmth and comfort.

God as light reminds me of the outposts of love all over the world. The light of Christ seems such a frail weapon against the powers of darkness that we may be tempted to trust in force and violence. But God assures us that the world's darkness can never put out his light.

The light shines in the darkness, and the darkness has never put it out—and never will. Alleluia!

 Father in heaven, Jesus the light of the world has scattered the darkness of hatred and sin. Called to that light, we become light. In this dark world, help us to let our light shine.

What images of God mean the most to you— shepherd, fire, spirit, the Way, or some others?

■ JOURNEY INTO THE UNKNOWN

Heb. 11:8-16: "By faith Abraham, when called to go to a place he would later receive as his inheritance, obeyed and went, even though he did not know where he was going" (v. 8).

Our life is a journey. We go from the known to the unknown, from the familiar and secure into a future we cannot see. We are pilgrims and sojourners, at times even lonely exiles.

Women today are moving into uncharted territory, with new problems and new opportunities. We have to make some choices that our mothers and grandmothers did not have to make.

We journey into the unknown, but we are not alone. We are sisters with all other women, seekers with every Christian. We have respect for others because they are wanderers too, and by sharing our struggles we help one another along the road.

The traditional past is not our home. This world is not our home. Here we have no "enduring city, but we are looking for the city that is to come." The world will continue to change, and women's issues will change. But as God's pilgrim people, we follow him as best we can, knowing he has prepared for us a city. We await the day when we are fully what we are meant to be. And we await the day when God's kingdom will fully come.

Lord, while we wait, may we make the world stronger by being ourselves, better by serving others and may we never forget that we belong to you.

List some of the challenging situations that you face. Ask yourself: "What is the worst, or best, that could happen?"